1001
Surprising Things
You Should Know
about God

Other titles by MacGregor and Prys:

1001 Surprising Things You Should Know about Christianity
1001 Surprising Things You Should Know about the Bible

1001
Surprising Things You Should Know about God

Jerry MacGregor & Marie Prys,
with Donna Wallace

Baker Books
A Division of Baker Book House Co
Grand Rapids, Michigan 49516

© 2003 by Jerry MacGregor and Marie Prys

Published by Baker Books
a division of Baker Publishing Group
P.O. Box 6287, Grand Rapids, MI 49516-6287
www.bakerbooks.com

Third printing, September 2004

Printed in the United States of America

Library of Congress Cataloging-in-Publication Data
MacGregor, Jerry.
    1001 Surprising things you should know about God / Jerry MacGregor
& Marie Prys.
        p.   cm.
    Includes bibliographical references.
    ISBN 0-8010-6449-X (pbk.)
    1. God—Miscellanea. I. Title: One thousand one things you should know about God. II. Title: One thousand and one things you should know about God. III. Prys, Marie. IV. Title.
    BT103 .M24 2003
    231—dc21   2002153412

Contents

Part III Putting It All Together

Introduction

"As fools long to play Shakespeare, so I have longed to write a book on God." These are the opening words of J. I. Packer's *Knowing God*. Of course, we wish we'd written them. The book you're holding in your hands probably won't take you down the same theological trail Packer does . . . but at least it should prove fun.

You see, we believe our God *is* fun. He is the creator of laughter, the originator of joy, and the God of surprises. It seems that everywhere you turn these days, people want to know God. We believe every individual was created with an innate desire to meet him. And the good news is that the Lord has *already* revealed himself to us clearly. Most of what we know about him is provided through his own words, as shared with us in the Bible. A careful reading of almost any passage of Scripture will reveal all sorts of insights into God—from his ancient plan to his present-day activities. All we have to do is open our eyes to the fact of God and we'll start to see him all around us. He has told us about his divine plan, his design for living, and his desire for our lives.

We therefore wrote this book in hopes of helping you know more about our God. *1001 Surprising Things You Should Know about*

God explores the character, actions, and events surrounding the one who authored life. This collection isn't made up of the 1001 "most important" facts about God, the 1001 "best" facts, or even the 1001 "most-necessary-for-a-complete-theological-education" facts. Instead we have tried to pick the unique, the important, and the unfamiliar things we think every person ought to know . . . or at least consider. We've combined them into a volume that, while perhaps never being selected for a seminary course, will at least be read for enjoyment and enlightenment by those who want to know God better.

We recognize that no humanly authored book can offer a complete picture of the Lord of the universe. But we pray this book will be used in some little way to offer you a better understanding of God, a greater appreciation of the immense nature of our creator. Get to know him and see if your life doesn't change.

                                          Jerry MacGregor and Marie Prys

Part I

Who God Is

1

All about God

1. Theism is the belief in a supernatural power or supernatural powers, in one or many gods. This view includes all the various beliefs in a god or gods and is opposed only to atheism. Theism is also used to describe the belief in the existence of but one God, whether personal or impersonal, whether presently active in the universe or not. Some theists believe in a personal God, both transcendent and immanent, and existing only in one person. This includes Jewish, Islamic, and Unitarian concepts of God. A fourth view is the most discriminating and the one we hold throughout this book—the belief in one personal God, both immanent and transcendent, who exists in three personal distinctions, known as

Father, Son, and Holy Spirit. This is Christian theism and is opposed to all the other views named.

2. The science of God and his works is called *theology.* This word is derived from two Greek words, *theos* and *logos,* the former meaning "God," and the latter, "word," "discourse," or "doctrine." In a narrow sense, theology may be defined as "the doctrine of God." However, in the broad and more usual sense, the term has come to mean all Christian doctrines that deal with the relations of God to the universe.

3. Theology has kept some pretty dry and dreary company, according to Dallas Willard in his book *Spirit of the Disciplines.* "We are tempted to leave it to the experts. But theology stands for something far too important to each of our individual lives and to the communities in which we live for us to shy away from it. Theology is an integral part of our lives. We each have one—whether thoughtless or carefully formed. Every Christian must strive to arrive at beliefs about God that faithfully reflect the realities of his or her life and experience."

4. Theology versus philosophy. Both theology and philosophy have the same basic objective—to seek a comprehensive worldview. However, they differ greatly in their approach to attaining this objective. While theology begins with the belief in the existence of God and the idea that he is the cause of all things, philosophy begins with the idea that it alone is sufficient to explain the existence of all other things. For some ancients, this explanation was water, air, or fire; for others it has been the mind or ideas; for still others, nature, personality, life, or some other thing. Theology does not merely begin with the belief in the existence of God but holds that he has graciously revealed himself. Philosophy denies both these ideas.

5. Reflecting on God, pastor Charles Spurgeon once noted, "He who often thinks of God, will have a larger mind than the man who simply plods around this narrow globe. . . . The most excellent study for expanding the soul, is the science of Christ, and Him crucified, and the knowledge of the Godhead in the glorious Trinity. Nothing will so enlarge the intellect, nothing so magnify the whole soul of man, as a devout, earnest, continued investigation of the great subject of the Deity."

6. The Christian God is omniscient, holy, loving, kind, and omnipotent. Being omniscient, he knows all about humanity's needs; since he is holy, he cannot excuse sin and take humanity in our fallen condition into fellowship with himself; because he is loving and kind, he may be moved to search for and put into operation a plan of salvation; and since he is omnipotent (all powerful), he not only reveals himself, but can also set forth in writing such revelations of himself as are needed for the experience of salvation.

7. *Deus Absconditus.* Blaise Pascal spoke of God as a *Deus Absconditus* (a hidden God), but he also held that this hidden God has revealed himself and therefore can be known.

8. The Bible and God. Because God is infinite, a comprehensive definition giving a complete and exhaustive portrayal of God is impossible. We can attempt to give a definition of God only as we know him and know *about* him as provided by Scripture.

9. The best summary of the doctrine of God as taught in the Bible is found in answer to question four of the *Westminster Shorter Catechism,* "What is God?" The answer: "God is a Spirit, infinite, eternal, and unchangeable, in his being, wisdom, power, holiness, justice, goodness, and truth." The great Charles Hodge described this statement as "the best definition of God ever penned by man."

10. Louis Berkhof's definition of God: "God is one, absolute, unchangeable and infinite in His knowledge and wisdom, His goodness and love, His grace and mercy, His righteousness and holiness."

11. In the Bible, life with God reads more like a mystery or a romance than a theology text. What is found in its pages differs markedly from what most people expect in getting to know God.

12. God is shy. The modern writer Philip Yancey describes God as shy, meaning not that he is bashful or timid, but rather that God shows incredible "self-restraint" even in things that displease him. After creating the world and the apex of his handiwork—humanity—God planned to enter into Sabbath rest when he and all his creatures would enjoy peace and harmony. Yet sin and history keep messing up his plan. Now God must set the pace of communication so we may know him when and how he wishes to make himself known.

13. God hides. Isaiah wrote, "Truly you are a God who hides himself" (45:15). Sometimes the Bible portrays God as the initiator, yet God sets a premium on his children living by faith, which can only be exercised in circumstances that allow for us to have doubts.

14. God is gentle. To describe God's gentle way of dealing with his children, contrast the possession of the Holy Spirit with that of an evil spirit described in the New Testament (Mark 9:18–21). Whenever the evil spirit seized the boy, he was thrown to the ground, his body rigid, teeth gnashing, and foaming at the mouth. God, on the other hand, humbles himself so deeply that he experiences emotional pain and suffering, so much that Paul has to warn his followers, "Quench not the Spirit" (1 Thess. 5:19 KJV) and "Grieve not the holy Spirit of God" (Eph. 4:30 KJV).

15. God is jealous. Jealousy is a strong emotion. The Song of Solomon likens it to love and compares its power to that of fire. Dan Allender and Tremper Longman set out to differentiate between godly jealousy and that which destroys. "Marriage is a mirror that reflects divine-human intimacy, and although this reflection is genuine, it is dim." As we may experience jealousy for our spouse, God feels it for his bride. But we must never lose sight of the difference between divine and human jealousy. God has the right to possess and protect. We do not possess our spouse, but *we do have the privilege of protecting* him or her.

16. God intends for us to feel righteous rage in order to mock the Evil One and destroy sin. Even though such rage appears to be the dark side of emotion, it bears the imprint of what God intended. As one modern writer puts it, "If we allow ourselves to join God's fury and then focus on what we are to hate—evil, sin, ugliness—our hearts may discover a new dimension of the character of God."

17. God has holy contempt. Contempt reflects something about the character of God that is often overlooked: God is a mocker. In fact, God does more than rage against arrogance; he plans on humiliating it. The psalmist writes, "The One enthroned in heaven laughs; the Lord scoffs at [those who rage against him]" (Ps. 2:4). "The wicked plot against the righteous and gnash their teeth at them; but the Lord laughs at the wicked, for he knows their day is coming" (Ps. 37:12–13).

18. The redemptive power of divine shame. Shame is an exposure of our idolatry because it reveals our foolish trust in ourselves. But it is also a great gift, because it is an invitation to grace. We encounter God's own humiliation in his Son's incarnation, earthly suffering, and crucifixion. Because God submitted to the shame of humility and lowliness, we are invited to enter into his humility by allowing our hearts to be grieved and broken through the exposure of sin.

19. He is a suffering God. "In all their affliction He was afflicted, and the angel of His presence saved them; in His love and in His mercy He redeemed them; and He lifted them and carried them all the days of old" (Isa. 63:9 NASB).

20. "The LORD longs to be gracious to you; he rises to show you compassion" (Isa. 30:18; cf. Gen. 21:15–17; 1 Samuel 1). Yet Scripture also says, "For it has been granted to you on behalf of Christ not only to believe on him, but also to suffer for him" (Phil. 1:29). Our call to suffer comes from a God tender beyond description.

21. Jesus' compassion drove him to open blind eyes and rouse lifeless limbs—he never glorified illness or eulogized pain and sorrow. But God's plan includes suffering. Despite Christ's compassionate death for our sins, God's plan calls for all Christians to suffer, sometimes intensely.

22. God is fully at peace. Only God is perfect in this. As a result, inner peace is not something we attain by eliminating pressure points or by the cessation of war or conflict. Rather, peace is allowing the perfectly integrated character of God to express himself through us.

23. The suffering God. When we read of Jeremiah mourning for his people, we see the heart of God through the words of his prophet: "Oh, that my head were a spring of water and my eyes a fountain of tears! I would weep day and night for . . . my people"

(Jer. 9:1). Hear the pain in God's heart when he pleads, "My people, what have I done to you? How have I burdened you?" (Micah 6:3). The pain described is that of a lover searching for the reason his people ignore his tender affection and protective love.

24. Frederick Buechner once wrote, "God puts Himself at our mercy not only in the sense of the suffering that we can cause Him by our blindness and coldness and cruelty, but the suffering that we can cause Him simply by suffering ourselves. Because that is the way love works, and when someone we love suffers, we suffer with him, and we would not have it otherwise because the suffering and the love are one, just as it is with God's love for us."

25. J. I. Packer challenges his readers to plug their ears to those who say there is no road to knowledge about God, and to travel a little way with him and see. "Anyone who is actually following a recognized road will not be too worried if he hears non-travelers telling each other that no such road exists."

26. We know God only through knowing Jesus Christ, who is himself God manifest in the flesh. Scripture makes this clear: "Hast thou not known me . . . ? he that hath seen me hath seen the Father." "No man cometh unto the Father, but by me" (John 14:9, 6 KJV). We must be clear in our minds as to what "knowing" Jesus Christ means.

2

What Is God Like?

27. Because God is infinite, a comprehensive definition providing a complete and exhaustive portrayal of God is impossible. However, we can give a definition of God insofar as we know him and know about him. The Bible reveals the attributes of God as revealed to humanity. We can say God is a being and then indicate the ways in which he is different from other beings.

28. God is with us. When considering the nature of God in relation to his created world, we usually speak of two concepts traditionally known as *transcendence* and *immanence*. Rather than exploring God's specific actions, these concepts regard his status in relationship to the world—the degree to which God is present and active within the universe.

29. Immanence. God is present and active within nature, human nature, and history. Jeremiah 23:24 emphasizes God's presence throughout the whole universe: "'Can anyone hide in secret places so that I cannot see him?' declares the LORD." The apostle Paul told the philosophers on Mars Hill, "Though he is not far from each one of us. 'For in him we live and move and have our being.' As some of your poets have said, 'We are his offspring'" (Acts 17:27–28).

30. Transcendence. The other aspect of the relationship of God to the world is the fact that he is separate from and independent of nature and humanity. God is not simply attached to or involved in his creation; he is superior in significant ways. "'For my thoughts are not your thoughts, neither are your ways my ways,' declares the LORD. 'As the heavens are higher than the earth, so are my ways higher than your ways and my thoughts than your thoughts'" (Isa. 55:8–9).

31. Kierkegaard once wrote, "The remarkable thing about the way in which people talk about God, or about their relation to God, is that it seems to escape them completely that God hears what they are saying. A man says, 'At the moment I have not the time or the necessary recollection to think about God, but later on perhaps.' Or better still a young man says, 'I am too young now; first of all I will enjoy life—and then.' Would it be possible to talk like that if one realized that God heard one?"

32. Philosophers and God. For Plato, God is the eternal mind, the cause of good in nature. Aristotle considered him to be "the first ground of all being." Benedict de Spinoza defined God as "the absolute, universal Substance, the real Cause of all and every existence: and not only the Cause of all being, but itself all being, of which every special existence is only a modification." Gottfried Leibniz said that the final reason of things is called God. Immanuel Kant defined God as a being who, by his understanding and will, is the cause of nature; a being who has all rights and no duties; the moral author of the world. For Johann Fichte, God was the moral order of the universe, actually operative in life. Georg Wilhelm Frederich Hegel considered God the absolute spirit, yet a spirit without consciousness until it becomes conscious in the reason and thoughts of man.

33. God is the infinite and perfect Spirit in whom all things have their source, support, and end, according to Strong's definition.

34. The existence of God is automatically assumed by the Scriptures. Because of this, the Bible does not attempt to prove his existence, rather it is assumed. The Scriptures begin with the majestic statement, "In the beginning God." Such texts as Psalm 94:9–23 and Isaiah 40:12–31 are not proofs of God's existence, but rather analytical accounts of all that is involved in the idea of God.

35. God is spirit. God is a substance. He is, however, not a material substance but a spiritual substance. Jesus said, "God is spirit" (John 4:24). Christ also said, "A spirit does not have flesh and bones as you see that I have" (Luke 24:39 NASB). The second commandment of the Decalogue, which forbids the making of any graven image or likeness of anything (Exod. 20:4), is based on the immaterial nature of God. So are the numerous commands against idolatry (see Lev. 26:1; Deut. 16:22).

36. God's body. What about the expressions that represent God as having bodily parts, such as hands, feet, eyes, and ears? These are anthropomorphic (assigning human form or character to God) and symbolic representations that serve to make God understandable and to express his various interests, powers, and activities.

37. God is infinite. God is spirit without beginning or end. Mankind is spirit, too, but differs in that we have a *finite* spirit, which is able to dwell in a material body (1 Cor. 2:11; 1 Thess. 5:23). God is infinite spirit and as such is without form (Acts 7:48).

38. God is invisible. God told Moses that no man could see him and live (Exod. 33:20). John says, "No one has seen God at any time" (John 1:18 NASB). Paul calls him "the invisible God" (Col. 1:15 NASB) and declares that no man has seen him or can see him (1 Tim. 6:16). Certain Scriptures, however, indicate that the redeemed will one day see God (Ps. 17:15; Matt. 5:8; Heb. 12:14; Rev. 22:4).

39. What about the Scriptures that say men saw God, such as Genesis 32:30; Exodus 3:6; 24:9–11; Numbers 12:6–8; Deuteronomy 34:10; and Isaiah 6:1? When one looks in a mirror, he or she in a sense sees oneself, yet does not literally see the true self. So men saw the reflection of God's glory, but they did not see his essence (Heb. 1:3). Then, too, spirit can be manifested in visible form (John 1:32). When Moses saw the "back" of God (Exod. 33:23), it was in response to his request to see the glory of the Lord (v. 18). Rather than literally and visibly seeing God, it is better understood that Moses saw the aftereffects of God.

40. Theophanies are manifestations of deity in visible form. After he had wrestled with the man, Jacob said, "I saw God face to face" (Gen. 32:30). "The angel of the Lord" was a visible manifestation of deity (Gen. 16:7–14; 18:13–33; 22:11–18; Exod. 3:2–5; Judg. 6:11–23; 1 Kings 19:5–7; 2 Kings 19:35). In some of these passages, "the angel of the Lord" is identified simply as "the Lord."

41. God is alive. The idea of spirit implies that God is not an inanimate substance but rather is alive. He is, therefore, called the "living" God (Josh. 3:10; 1 Sam. 17:26; Ps. 84:2; Matt. 16:16; 1 Tim. 3:15; Rev. 7:2). Life implies feeling, power, and activity. God has all of these (Ps. 115:3). He is also the source and support of all life: plant, animal, human, spiritual, and eternal (Ps. 36:9; John 5:26). The living God is always in contrast to dead idols (Ps. 115:3–9; Acts 14:15; 1 Thess. 1:9). Our God is alive. He sees, hears, and loves.

42. God is a person. The only way of determining what spirit is like, apart from Scriptures, is by analogy with the human spirit. Since the human spirit is personal, the Divine Spirit must be personal as well, for otherwise he is of a lower order of being than humanity. What is the essence of personality? Self-consciousness and self-determination.

43. God is self-conscious and self-determinative. As conscious beings, we often think spontaneously, but do not always think about those thoughts. As *self*-conscious beings, however, we can relate and reflect on our personal feelings, appetites, and thoughts. Likewise, *self*-determination is more than determination. Humans have the feeling of freedom, are able to make choices, and can consider our motives and ends. The Scripture writers also ascribe both self-consciousness (Exod. 3:14; Isa. 45:5; 1 Cor. 2:10) and self-determination (Job 23:13; Rom. 9:11; Eph. 1:9, 11; Heb. 6:17) to God.

44. God has personality. The Bible reveals that God has intellect (Gen. 18:19; Exod. 3:7; Acts 15:18), sensibility (Gen. 6:6; Ps.

103:8–14; John 3:16), and volition (Gen. 3:15; Ps. 115:3; John 6:38). Furthermore, it ascribes qualities and relations of personality to God. He is represented as speaking (Gen. 1:3), seeing (Gen. 11:5), hearing (Ps. 94:9), grieving (Gen. 6:6), and repenting (Gen. 6:6); and being angry (Deut. 1:37), jealous (Exod. 20:5), and compassionate (Ps. 111:4). He is said to be the creator (Acts 14:15), upholder (Neh. 9:6), ruler (Ps. 75:7; Dan. 4:32), and sustainer of all things (Ps. 104:27–30; Matt. 6:26–30).

45. The Bible calls him "the blessed God" (1 Tim. 1:11). Ancient Greeks used the word *blessed* to describe the rich and powerful—society's upper crust—and to label the gods, who could have whatever they wanted and do as they pleased.

46. God is self-existent. While humanity's ground of existence is outside ourselves, God's existence is not dependent upon anything outside himself. As Thomas Aquinas said, "He is the first cause, Himself uncaused." His self-existence is implied in his affirmation, "I AM WHO I AM" (Exod. 3:14).

47. God is immense. God is infinite in relation to space. He is not limited or bound by space; on the contrary, all finite space is dependent on him. He is, in fact, above space. Scripture clearly teaches God's immensity (1 Kings 8:27; 2 Chron. 2:6; Pss. 113:4–6; 139:7–12; Isa. 66:1; Jer. 23:24; Acts 17:24–28). Due to the spirituality of his nature and our inability to think in spaceless terms, God's immensity is a difficult doctrine to comprehend. God is both immanent and transcendent, and he is everywhere present in essence as well as in knowledge and power.

48. God is eternal. God is infinite in relation to time. He is without beginning or end, is free from all succession of time, and is the cause of time. He is called "the Everlasting God" (Gen. 21:33 NASB). The psalmists say, "From everlasting to everlasting, thou art God" (Ps. 90:2 KJV) and "Thou art the same, and thy years shall have no end" (Ps. 102:27 KJV). Isaiah represents God as "the high and exalted One Who lives forever" (Isa. 57:15 NASB). Paul says that God "alone possesses immortality" (1 Tim. 6:16 NASB).

49. Gregory the Great once said, "God is within all things, but not included; outside all things, but not excluded; above all things, but not beyond their reach."

50. Eternity for God is one "now," one eternal present. In Scripture this is referred to as "the day of eternity" (2 Peter 3:18 NASB) and "today" (Ps. 2:7). God sees the past and the future as vividly as he sees the present. In other words, a person may view a procession from the top of a high tower, seeing the whole procession at one glance, or he or she may view it from the street corner, where only one part can be seen at a time. God sees the whole as one unit, although he is aware of the sequence in the procession.

51. God is the cause of time. The reference to God in Isaiah 9:6 may be translated "Father of Eternity." Both time and space are among "all things" that "came into being through him" (John 1:3 NRSV). Time will someday merge into eternity (1 Cor. 15:28).

52. All contentment is a foretaste of eternity where "God himself will be with them and be their God. He will wipe every tear from their eyes. There will be no more death or mourning or crying or pain, for the old order of things has passed away" (Rev. 21:3–4).

53. God is unified. The unity of God means that there is one God and that the divine nature is undivided and indivisible. "Hear, O Israel! The LORD is our God, the LORD is one!" (Deut. 6:4 NASB). That there is but one God is the great truth of the Old Testament (Deut. 4:35, 39; 1 Kings 8:60; Isa. 45:5–6). The same truth is frequently taught in the New Testament (Mark 12:29–32; John 17:3). Unity implies that the three persons of the Trinity are not separate within the divine essence.

54. God is not merely one, he is the *only* God. Only one infinite and perfect being exists. The unity of God allows for personal distinctions in the divine nature, while at the same time recognizing that the divine nature is *numerically* and *eternally* One.

3

His Names

55. God in the plural. It is interesting that God used plural pronouns (Gen. 1:26; 3:22; 11:7; Isa. 6:8) and plural verbs (Gen. 1:26; 11:7) to refer to himself. The name for God *(Elohim)* is plural—though this form is most likely used for intensity.

56. Biblical names of persons and places carry great significance, a fact that is especially true with the names for deity. In biblical times, a name represented a person's character. God's name not only represents his character but his attributes and his nature as well. To know his name is *to know him.* To boast in his name is to have confidence in who he is (Ps. 20:7).

57. That I may know him. Jesus' prayer on our behalf just before he went to the cross was, "That they may know thee the only true God, and Jesus Christ whom thou hast sent" (John 17:3 KJV). Paul also states the ultimate goal in life, "That I may know him" (Phil. 3:10 KJV). Unfortunately, we often miss the multifaceted aspects of God's nature in translation.

58. Describing God. As it takes many rays to make up the pure light of the sun, it takes many varied descriptions to give us a true conception of the being and glory of God. No finite person is able to receive the whole revelation of his majesty at once. Only one part at a time can be comprehended. God carefully orchestrated ways to reveal himself with different names and titles describing his nature and purpose so that we may know him.

59. The Law of First Mention. In Bible study, it is important to keep in mind what Dr. A. T. Pierson calls *The Law of First Mention.* Often the first mention of a person, place, doctrine, or word is an "embryo of a feature or a fact that will develop further." This idea applies to almost all the divine names and titles in Scripture.

60. God. The fourth word in the opening of the Bible is the first mentioned name in the Bible—"In the beginning God . . ." (Gen. 1:1). This first verse is his signature, suggesting that the book holy men would write under his inspiration belonged to him.

EL

61. El, with its derivations Elim, Elohim, and Eloah, is similar to the Greek *theos,* the Latin *Deus,* and the English *God.* This is one of the oldest and most widely distributed terms for deity known to the human race and is used to include all members of the class of deity. This short title is the most primitive Semitic name; its root meaning is most likely "to be strong," "might," or "power" (even when it's not used for God, it is still translated "might" or "power" [Gen. 31:29; Deut. 28:32]).

62. The poetical name. In classical Hebrew, *El* is mainly poetical. While found throughout the Old Testament, it is discovered more often in Job and the Psalms than in other books. *El* is also one of the names given to the promised Messiah, *El*, the mighty (Isa. 9:6–7).

63. *Eloi, Eloi.* In the New Testament crucifixion narrative, Jesus cried out in a loud voice, *"Eloi, Eloi"* (Mark 15:34). In his extreme weakness, he prayed "my strength, my strength," as he cried out for *El*, "the Strong One—the first and only cause of things." This moment was predicted hundreds of years earlier in Psalm 22 (called the Calvary Psalm). Christ pleads to *El* in his agony, "My God, My God, why have you forsaken me?"

64. *El* is found in ancient compound proper names such as Isra-*el*, Beth-*el*, *El*-elohe-*el*, meaning "House of Israel," Peni-*el*, face of *El*, Prince of *El*, *El* Shaddai. This two-letter name can also be found in all biblical names commencing with El, such as Eliakim, Elihu, Elimelech, Elisha, and Elizabeth.

65. Throughout the Bible, *Elohim* usually refers to God (found some three thousand times—over twenty-three hundred of which are applied to God). Though *Elohim* is the primary word translated "God" in the Old Testament, it can also be used of pagan deities or gods. For instance, it is used for idols (Exod. 34:17), men (Ps. 82:6; John 10:34–35), angels (Pss. 8:5; 97:7), god-men (Gen. 3:5), and judges (Exod. 22:8). In these instances, the idea of might and authority are communicated by the word. Deuteronomy 10:17 says, "For the LORD your God *[Elohim]* is God of gods. . . ."

66. *Elohim*—Creator. The name *Elohim* primarily designates God as God. The plural ending, *him*, is especially significant in Hebrew because it indicates three. *Elohim*, the name for God as creator, is used in Genesis 1:1 and thus could be translated, "In the beginning *Gods* created the heavens and the earth." (In the first two chapters of Genesis, *Elohim* occurs thirty-five times in connection with God's creative power.)

67. The plural *Elohim* does not mean there was more than one God. Rather, the Old Testament writers used the name with singular verbs and adjectives to denote a singular idea. "The LORD [Jehovah] our God *[Elohim]*, the LORD is one" (Deut. 6:4). God the Father, God the Son, and God the Holy Spirit created the heavens and the earth. One in essence and in character; yet three persons united as one.

68. Each person in the Godhead had a part in creation. In various parts of Scripture, you can see the different persons of the Godhead participating in the work of creation. In Genesis 1:2–3 we read, "the Spirit of God was moving over the surface of the waters. Then God said, 'Let there be light'; and there was light" (NASB). God spoke, the Spirit moved, and Colossians 1:16 tells us that in him, Christ Jesus, the Son of God, "all things were created, both in the heavens and on earth." This is also seen in the creation of man. In Genesis 1:26, we read, "Then God *[Elohim]* said, 'Let us make man in our image.'"

69. The maker and keeper of covenant. The idea conveyed by *Elohim* is always that of one in a covenant relationship. In his words to Abram, *Elohim's* name pledges this relationship: "I am the Almighty God; walk before me, and be thou perfect. . . . And I will establish my covenant between me and thee and thy seed after thee in their generations . . . and I will be their" *Elohim,* that is, I will be with them in covenant relationship (Gen. 17:1–8 KJV).

70. "I am the LORD your God, . . . you are precious and honored in my sight, . . . everyone who is called by my name, whom I created for my glory, whom I formed and made" (Isa. 43:3–4, 7). The word for "glory" in Greek is *doxa,* and it means to give the correct opinion or estimate of. We have been created for God's glory—to give all of creation a correct opinion or estimate of who God is.

71. *Elah, Eloah*—the Adorable One. *Elah* is the Chaldee form of *Eloah,* which is known as a verbal noun, and is associated with the Hebrew verb *alah,* meaning to fear, to worship, to adore. The Adorable One. This distinctive divine name stands for the nature and expression of the only living and true God, the object of all testimony and worship. David asked, "Who is *[Eloah]* besides the LORD?" (2 Sam. 22:32). God asks, "Is there any *[Eloah]* besides me?" (Isa. 44:8).

72. One of the oldest names for God is "Redeemer." In faith Job proclaimed, "I know that my Redeemer lives, and that in the end he will stand upon the earth. And after my skin has been destroyed, yet in my flesh I will see God" (19:25–26). *Eloah,* the one we worship and adore.

73. *Eloah*—Absolute Deity. As in *Elohim* we have unity in the Trinity, so in *Eloah* we have absolute Deity. Both the Old and New Testaments emphasize, "The LORD our God is one Lord."

74. The first occurrence of *Elah* is in Ezra 4:24 where it is used in connection with the work of rebuilding "the house of God" *(Elah)*. This divine title occurs some ninety times in the Old Testament—forty-three times in Ezra, forty-six times in Daniel, and once in Jeremiah 10:10. *Elah* indicates that the living and true God is identified with his people in captivity. The word *Elah* means an oak—the tree symbolizing durability—a virtue characteristic of him who is "the Everlasting God."

75. *El Elyon*—the Most High God. The compound *El-Elyon* designates God as the highest, the most high (Ps. 78:35). He is the sovereign ruler over all the universe. It was *El Elyon,* "God Most High, who delivered" Abraham's enemies into his hand (Gen. 14:20). It was the Most High God who was and is the Redeemer of Israel (Ps. 78:35). And it is the Most High God who rules today over the affairs of men (Dan. 4:34–35). Although humanity has been given a free will, God still overrules so that no man, angel, demon, devil, or any circumstance of life can thwart his plan.

76. The Highest in Order. Several names for God are applied in Scripture to things and persons of the world. *Elyon,* for instance, was a name used by other nations than Israel. But wherever it is used, the person or thing it speaks of is the highest of a series or order of "like natures." When applied to God, *Elyon* or "Most High" reveals that though he is the highest, others below him are endowed with like natures, and are therefore in some way related to him.

77. *Theos.* In the New Testament, the term *theos* takes the place of *El, Elohim,* and *Elyon.* The names *Shaddai* and *El Shaddai* are rendered *pantokrator,* the almighty, and *theos pantokrator,* God almighty. Sometimes the Lord is called "the Alpha and the Omega" (Rev. 1:8), "who is, and who was, and who is to come" (Rev. 1:4), "the First and the Last" (Rev. 2:8), and "the Beginning and the End" (Rev. 21:6).

78. *El-Elohe-Israel*—God of Israel. Jacob gave this name to the altar he erected at Shalem (Gen. 33:18–20). Jacob's act of faith, allocating his new name, Israel, also claims *Elohim.* Only with God could Israel walk according to his new name. (When God's name is connected to human names, it communicates that the bearer of the name experienced a new revelation of God's character and purpose, such as the God of Abraham, the God of Isaac, the God of Jacob, etc.)

79. *El Olam*—God of Eternity. A rare title in Scripture, *El Olam* describes what extends beyond our farthest vision, whether looking forward or backward, to instill a sense of purpose. Such reason is found in the God of Eternity, or as the KJV translates it, "the Everlasting God." Any time this name occurs, a reference (sometimes more hidden) is made to the distinct stages of God's dealings with his people through his eternal wisdom.

80. The first occurrence of the name *El Olam* carries heavy spiritual significance. It is found in connection with Abraham's struggle with Abimelech over the right to use wells. God caused Abraham to wander for many years, until at last he felt as if he could settle in the pastures near the streams of Beersheba. But the men of Gerar wanted to oust him. It was at this time that *El Olam,* God the Everlasting, revealed himself to Abraham, reminding him of an everlasting purpose (Gen. 20:13).

81. *El Roi*—the God who sees. Have you ever been unjustly turned away or thrown out, perhaps abandoned? Perhaps you fulfilled someone's pleasure and then you weren't wanted anymore. Maybe you have a child who has run away. Deep in your heart you may wonder if you failed in some way or were inadequate. Divorces, company layoffs, affairs, thefts . . . where is God? Does he know what is going on? The omnipresent God is there with you, and he sees all. Healing begins with a God who saw it all. We can trust in righteous judgment because he is *El Roi;* he saw it all (2 Thess. 1:5–10).

82. The only occurrence of the title *El Roi* in Scripture is in connection with Hagar's flight from Sarah. Out in the wilderness of Shur, God spoke to Sarah's handmaid, instructing her to return. Hagar had borne the son of Sarah's husband, Abraham (Genesis 16), and then was terribly mistreated. *El Roi* accompanies us as we turn back and face our oppressors. Writes the psalmist, "Where can I go from your Spirit? Where can I flee from your presence?" (Ps. 139:7).

83. *El Shaddai*—the Almighty, All-Sufficient One. The translation of the Hebrew word *Shaddai* is not totally clear in its meaning because scholars are not absolutely sure of its root word, but many believe it is a designation of God as the All-Sufficient One.

84. The first mention of the all-sufficient nature of God comes during a solemn occasion when God appeared to Abram and opened his message to the patriarch with "I am the Almighty God" (Gen. 17:1 KJV). When the Lord appeared, ninety-nine-year-old Abram fell on his face before God (Gen. 17:1–3). *El Shaddai*, the All-Sufficient One, made a covenant with the new father of nations and changed his name to Abraham. The same title was used when God appeared to Jacob and Isaac to bless them. In God all fullness dwells, and out of his constant fullness, his own receive all things.

85. *Shaddai*. The thought expressed in this name for God describes power, not of violence but of all-bountifulness. *Shaddai* primarily means "breasted," being formed directly from the Hebrew word *shad,* that is, "the breast," or more precisely, a woman's breast. Lewis G. Parkhust explains the divine title or name *Shaddai* as "'The Pourer or Shedder forth,' One that Satisfies with blessings both physical and spiritual." "Can a woman forget her nursing child, and have no compassion [tenderness] on the son of her womb? Even these may forget, but I will not forget you" (Isa. 49:15 NASB).

86. *Sheddim,* the kindred name to *Shaddai,* refers to objects of idolatrous worship in other parts of Scripture and describes the many-breasted idols, representing the genial powers of nature, which were worshiped among the heathen as givers of rain and bounty. *El Shaddai* is the true Giver of Life—even of his own life, of whom these heathen *Sheddim* were the idolatrous perversion.

87. *Adonai*—Lord Master/Ruler is a title that appears frequently in the prophets, expressing humanity's dependence and submission, as of a servant to his master or a wife to her husband. The title, Lord of Hosts, appears frequently in the prophetical and postexilic literature (Isa. 1:9; 6:3 NRSV). Some take the term to refer to God's presence with the armies of Israel in the times of the monarchy (1 Sam. 4:4; 17:45; 2 Sam. 6:2), but a more probable meaning is

God's presence with the hosts of heaven, the angels (Ps. 89:6–8; cf. James 5:4).

88. *Adonai* is a title that heathen nations applied to their gods. The Greek word comes from the Phoenician word *adon,* which means "lord." In Scripture it is often compounded with Jehovah as a proper name as, for instance, in *Adoni-jah,* which means "Jehovah is Lord." *Baal* was also used, which implies master or owner.

89. *Baal.* While we think of *Baal* as the title of the Canaanite local gods, in earlier times it was actually used by worshipers of God. For this reason, one of Saul's sons was named Ish-baal. One of David's men of war was known as Baaliah, which means, "Jehovah is Baal." When this title came to have degrading associations, proper names were changed and *Baal* became *Bosheth,* which was substituted in names such as Ishbosheth.

JEHOVAH

90. The Name of God. "He that blasphemeth the name of the Lord, he shall surely be put to death" (Lev. 24:16 KJV). In response to the Old Testament Law, every Jew became so alarmed at the danger connected with the pronouncing or writing of this wonderful name that they dared not give expression to it for fear that the stroke of God might come upon them for uttering, and possibly blaspheming, the incomprehensible, or what might be called, *the* name of God.

91. *Jehovah* or *Yahweh*—the Eternal, Ever-Loving One. This is the personal name par excellence of Israel's God. The term is connected with the Hebrew verb "to be," and means the "self-existent one," or the "one who causes to be." This name is often translated into the English version by the word "Lord," using capital and small capital letters.

92. *Jehovah* is the most frequently used of all the different names of God in the Old Testament (appearing about seven thousand times). Its meaning is "God of the covenant." The first usage occurs in Genesis, where *Jehovah* is compounded with *Elohim.*

93. Among all the divine names none is so solemn as *Jehovah.*
Rabbinical writings have distinguished *Jehovah* by such euphemistic
expressions as "*the* Name," "the Great and Terrible Name," "the
Peculiar Name," "the Separate Name," "the Unutterable Name,"
"the Ineffable Name," "the Incommunicate Name," "the Holy
Name," and "the Distinguished Name." It was also known as "the
Name of Four Letters" because when taken from the Hebrew it is
spelled YHVH in English. Such Jewish reverence remains today—so
much so that many refrain from writing it or pronouncing it.

94. At the time of the covenant, God gave something to Abram,
which at once changed him from Abram to Abraham. What God
adds is the letter *he,* the chief letter of his own name *Jehovah*—that
sound which can only be uttered by an out-breathing—thus giving to the elect something of his own nature (remember, a name
denotes nature).

95. The meaning of this ancient name, which is said to be whis-
pered only by the high priest in the Holy of Holies once a year, is
perhaps most adequately described in the Book of Revelation. The
absoluteness of the divine, who is independent and self-existent,
is found in the declaration "I am Alpha and Omega, the beginning
and the ending, saith the Lord *[Jehovah]* which is, and which was,
and which is to come, the Almighty" (Rev. 1:8 KJV).

96. *Jehovah* **means "I AM WHO I AM."** At the burning bush,
Moses "said to God, 'Behold, I am going to the sons of Israel, and
I will say to them, "The God of your fathers has sent me to you."
Now they may say to me, "What is His name?" What shall I say
to them?' God said to Moses, 'I AM WHO I AM;' and He said, 'Thus
you shall say to the sons of Israel, "I AM has sent me to you." . . .
"The LORD, the God of your fathers, the God of Abraham, the God
of Isaac, and the God of Jacob, has sent me to you." This is My
name forever, and this is My memorial-name to all generations'"
(Exod. 3:13–15 NASB).

97. The name *Jehovah* **is derived from the archaic** *havah,*
which means "to be, to become." Jehovah speaks of God's being
or essence. When we read the name of Jehovah, or LORD in capital
and small capital letters in our Bible, we should think in terms of
being, or existence and life, and we must think of Jehovah as the

being who is absolutely self-existent, the one who in himself possesses essential life and permanent existence.

98. JAH—the Independent One. JAH, which is pronounced "ya," is a shortened form of *Jehovah.* This name signifies that *he is,* and can be made to correspond to I AM, just as *Jehovah* corresponds to the fuller expression I AM THAT I AM. The name first appears in the triumphal Song of Moses in Exodus 15. We also see the combination, "JAH Jehovah is my strength and my song," where both present and future deliverance are implied (Isa. 12:2).

99. JAH is the present tense of the verb "to be". It suggests Jehovah as the *present* living God—the presence of God in daily life, or his present activity. JAH is "an ever-*present* help in trouble" (Ps. 46:1, emphasis added). Most people miss the connection with the often-repeated exclamation, "Praise ye the Lord," also meaning, "Praise ye JAH," or "Hallelu*jah.*"

100. JAH in human names. JAH, the shortened form of *Jehovah,* is interwoven like other divine names with human names, always with a particular purpose and meaning. Many more names contain JAH at the end than at the beginning, most likely to show reverence. For example, Abi*jah* means "whose father is Jehovah."

101. God's title, JAH, is found in Psalm 68:4: "Extol him that rideth upon the heavens by his name [JAH], and rejoice before him" (KJV). The same Hebrew word occurs over forty times in Isaiah, the Psalms, and Exodus but is translated "the Lord" in our English Bible. Regrettably, the various titles of God have not been given their Hebrew significance in translation.

102. Jehovah occurs in a number of powerful combinations. *Jehovah-Jireh,* the Lord will provide (Gen. 22:14); *Jehovah-Rapha,* the Lord that heals (Exod. 15:26); *Jehovah-Nissi,* the Lord is my banner (Exod. 17:15); *Jehovah-Shalom,* the Lord is peace (Judg. 6:24); *Jehovah-Raah,* the Lord is my shepherd (Ps. 23:1); *Jehovah-Tsidqenu,* the Lord our righteousness (Jer. 23:6); and *Jehovah-Shammah,* the Lord is present (Ezek. 48:35).

103. *Jehovah-Eloheenu*—the LORD *Our* God. Nineteen times this expression is given in the Book of Deuteronomy. It is a title suggesting the *commonwealth* of God's people in him (Ps. 99:5, 8–9).

From references in Deuteronomy, we learn what he is (6:4), where he is (4:7), what he said (1:6, 19; 2:37; 5:25, 27), what he did (2:33, 36; 3:3; 23:14), what he gave (1:20, 25), what he has (29:29), and what he shows (5:24).

104. *Jehovah-Eloheka*—the Lord *Thy* God. This title is closely related to *Jehovah-Eloheenu* (though it's more personal) and likewise occurs frequently in Deuteronomy, being found in chapter 16 twenty times. Often used in the Book of Exodus, this divine name describes Jehovah's relationship to his people and focuses more on their responsibility to him.

105. *Jehovah-Elohai*—the Lord *My* God. This name can be linked to *Adon* or *Adonai,* a personal name meaning *my Lord,* and likewise emphasizing divine sovereignty (Judg. 6:15; 13:8). *Elohai* specifically points to the personal pronoun "my" as being expressive of a personal faith in the God of power (Zech. 14:5). Though he is God of his people, we can know him—all that he is in himself and all his blessings on us personally.

106. *Jehovah-Hoseenu*—the Lord Our Maker. In Psalm 95:6, the writer invites us to join him in approaching the throne of God, "Come, let us bow down in worship, let us kneel before the LORD our Maker." The Hebrew word *asah* is used to speak about God in a variety of ways as our maker. When this term is applied to Jehovah as our maker, the reference is not to his work at creation when he spoke things into being, but rather to his ability to fashion something out of what already exists. Paul reminds us that "we are his workmanship."

107. *Jehovah-Jireh*—the Lord Will Provide. This name stands as a monument of a great discovery and a remarkable deliverance in Genesis 22. The story of Abraham and Isaac introduces the God who sees and provides. For death there is only one provider, *Jehovah-Jireh.* Jehovah, who in himself possesses essential life, is the only one who can make provision for sinful man to live, and he does it by providing the Lamb of God who takes away the sins of the world.

108. *Jehovah-Jireh*—"Sees all of our needs." The word for provide, *jireh,* in the Old Testament means literally to see. How do the words *see* and *provide* relate? Because of his omniscience and perfection of character, God not only sees, he foresees. And *Jehovah-Jireh* provides for, or supplies, whatever the foreseen need may be. The seeing or providing of the ram was what caused Abraham to name that place "The LORD Will Provide. And to this day it is said, 'On the mountain of the LORD it will be provided'" or "it will be seen" (Gen. 22:14).

109. *Jehovah-Jireh*—**The Provider of Our Salvation/Mount Moriah** (provides for both life and death). *Moriah*, in the Hebrew, is a kindred word to *Jireh*, taken from "Jehovah seeing," and can be translated "seen of JAH," or "the vision of Jehovah." Not only was Mount Moriah the location where Abraham offered Isaac, but it was also the site on which Solomon would build the house of the Lord in Jerusalem (2 Chron. 3:1). Down through the ages, at Mount Moriah every temple sacrifice for sin would echo Abraham's words, "The LORD Will Provide *[Jehovah-Jireh]*" (Gen. 22:14).

110. *Jehovah-Meqoddishkem* **(or** *M'Qaddesh***)—the Lord Who Sanctifies You.** God brought his people to Mount Sinai where he gave them the covenant of the Law and the pattern of the tabernacle where they would worship their God. These commandments would set them apart for God's own possession. Here they would come to know Jehovah as *Jehovah-Meqoddishkem* through observing his Sabbaths (Exod. 31:12–18).

111. The words *sanctify, set apart, holy,* **and** *saint* all come from a common root word, *qadash* in the Hebrew and *hagios* in the Greek. For the first time in Scripture, at Mount Sinai the purpose of the command for the Sabbath is laid out before the children of Israel. The Sabbath is to be a sign between God and Israel throughout all their generations so "that you may know that I am the LORD who sanctifies you" (Exod. 31:13 NASB). As God made the Sabbath holy to the children of Israel, he made the children of Israel holy, or set apart, unto himself.

112. As God sanctified Israel, he sanctifies the church. Holiness is not an option for believers, rather it is part of a perpetual covenant . . . a sign between God and the sons of Israel forever. "By this will we have been sanctified through the offering of the body of Jesus Christ once for all" (Heb. 10:10 NASB; see also John 17:15–19; 1 Thess. 4:3–8; 5:23).

113. The correct pronunciation of JHWH, the original name of God, has been lost. After a certain time, no knowledge remained of the way in which Jehovah should be pronounced. When Jewish scribes were writing out the Scriptures and came to the name of Jehovah, the Awful One, they would in most cases not write it as originally given, but would write the less awful name of *Adonai*, meaning, *"my Ruler."*

THE BANNER

114. *Jehovah-Nissi*—the Lord My Banner first appears in Exodus 17 at verse 8 with this significant statement: "Then Amalek came and fought against Israel" (NASB). Amalek, the grandson of Esau, was the first and constant enemy of Israel. And there would be no white flag of surrender in this battle. Amalek was an enemy of God and had to be subdued. In this famous battle, God was first worshiped as *Jehovah-Nissi,* "The LORD is my Banner" (Exod. 17:15). When Moses held up his hands, Israel prevailed, but when his arms grew weak and fell, Amalek would begin to conquer.

115. A banner was an ensign or standard carried at the head of a military band to indicate the line of march or the rallying point. A banner in ancient times was not necessarily a flag such as we use today. Often it was a bare pole with a bright shining ornament that glittered in the sun. The word *nissi* has interesting implications: as a *standard* (Isa. 5:26), as a *sign* (Num. 26:10), and as a *pole* in connection with the brazen serpent lifted up upon it to give life to Israel. Our Savior was lifted up on the pole, and by all he accomplished, we have victory.

116. The fearless and courageous Joshua came to the front in God's war against Amalek. He had a name that in its Hebrew form means Jesus—"I will be salvation." Isaiah prophesied that "the Root of Jesse will stand as a banner for the peoples" and one around which the Gentiles and Israel would rally (Isa. 11:10, 12).

117. A monument was built to celebrate this glorious deliverance from Amalek. Moses built an altar and called it *Jehovah-Nissi,* or Jehovah my Banner. Moses took care to give God the glory.

Although the name *Jehovah-Nissi* appears only here on the memorial altar, the truth it expresses runs throughout Scripture.

118. *Jehovah-Qanna.* When God gave the Ten Commandments, he said, "I am the LORD your God, who brought you out of Egypt, out of the land of slavery. You shall have no other gods before me. . . . You shall not bow down to them or worship them; for I, the LORD your God, am a jealous God" (Exod. 20:1–5). Again in Exodus 34:12–17, God tells his people not to make covenant with the inhabitants of the land into which they were going because "the LORD, whose name is Jealous, is a jealous God" (v. 14).

119. Holy jealousy. A holy and godly jealousy is rooted in divine love (2 Cor. 11:2), and God acts according to his name just as he has warned his people he will. His people acted like harlots in their worship of idols and other gods, and God kept his promise—his presence left Jerusalem (Ezra 8:3–6, 17–18; 9:9–10).

120. God's Word stands above and according to his name. Although God's presence withdrew from Jerusalem, God came back because he is a God of covenant (promise). God was jealous for his holy name, but his Word stands above or according to his name, so he would return in his glory to Jerusalem, though his children would have to wait approximately six hundred years. He returned as the Messiah, but most of Israel did not recognize him. He came to his own, but his own received him not (John 1:11).

HEALER AND SHEPHERD

121. *Jehovah-Rapha (Rophi)*—the Lord That Heals. "Is there no balm in Gilead? Is there no physician there?" (Jer. 8:22). *Rapha* means "to mend," as a garment is mended, "to repair" as a building is reconstructed, and "to cure" as a diseased person is restored to health. The psalmist wrote, "who . . . heals all your diseases" (Ps. 103:3). In Ezekiel, the Hebrew word for "heal" is translated as "physician" (30:21). *Jehovah-Rapha* also heals a distressed nation or person by restoring them to prosperous circumstances; healing in a moral sense, curing the mind and pardoning the soul.

122. The children of Israel needed a healer. Soon after God delivered Israel, they needed him as *Jehovah-Rapha*. As Moses led his people from the Red Sea into the wilderness of Shur, they found no water. When they came to Marah they couldn't drink because the water was bitter. The people grumbled. When Moses cried out to the Lord, God showed him a tree to throw into the waters and they became sweet. God then tested his people, saying, "If you will give earnest heed to the voice of the LORD your God, . . . I will put none of the diseases on you which I have put on the Egyptians; for I, the LORD, am your healer" (Exod. 15:26).

123. "Heal me, O Lord." Whether it is the illness of a nation or of a single human being, it is God who heals lands, pestilences, bodies, emotions, souls, and spirits. He may use other humans as his instruments, but they are useless without the Physician's power to heal. Whenever one needs healing, he or she must first consult *Jehovah-Rapha*. "Heal me, O LORD, and I shall be healed; save me, and I shall be saved: for thou art my praise" (Jer. 17:14).

124. The term *heal* is used:

- to express God's grace in restoring spiritual life—he heals all our diseases, spiritual as well as physical (Ps. 103:3).
- to heal the broken in heart (Ps. 147:3).
- to recover the faithless from backsliding (Jer. 3:22).
- to remove bodily sickness or disease (Gen. 20:17; 2 Kings 20:5).

125. *Jehovah-Raah (Rohi)*—the Lord my Shepherd. This name has several meanings, all suggesting the many aspects of Jehovah's care. For example, it can be translated "feeder, keeper" (Gen. 4:2), "companion" (Prov. 28:7), "friend" (Judg. 14:20), "pastor" (Jer. 17:16), "herdsman" (Gen. 13:7), and "shepherd" (Ps. 23:1).

126. Pastoral people of the Bible lands are familiar with the life and caring role of a shepherd and the utter dependence of sheep on their shepherd. Many have found great comfort knowing God thinks and cares for us as sheep. "We all, like sheep, have gone astray" (Isa. 53:6). "My sheep hear my voice" (John 10:27). "We are . . . sheep of his pasture" (Ps. 100:3 NRSV). "I . . . will search for My sheep and seek them out" (Ezek. 34:11 NASB). "Feed my sheep"

(John 21:17). Many Scriptures refer to God as our shepherd and to us as his sheep (John 10:1–17, 26–30).

127. The Twenty-third Psalm opens by summarizing one of the greatest truths concerning what it means to be a child of God—to have him as our *Jehovah-Raah.* "The LORD is my shepherd; I shall not want" (KJV). The rest of the psalm describes why there is no want for those whose shepherd is Jehovah.

128. "He maketh me to lie down" (v. 2). Here the psalmist is not describing a shepherd who forces his sheep to rest, but rather he is saying that because the shepherd has met all the flock's needs, it can lie down. According to Phillip Keller, it is impossible for a sheep to lie down unless four things are true:

- First, sheep must be free from hunger. They cannot lie down as long as they feel a need for finding food. In the second verse of Psalm 23, the Shepherd has so satisfied the sheeps' hunger that they can lie down in the midst of green pastures.
- Second, if sheep are to rest, they must be free of fear. Sheep are helpless, timid animals with little self-defense, and they are easily frightened.
- Third, sheep cannot rest unless they are free from friction. Tension with other sheep keeps them on their feet. They feel they must defend themselves.
- Fourth, sheep cannot rest unless they are free from pests like flies, parasites, or things that torment them.

THE GOD OF PEACE

129. *Jehovah-Sabaoth* **(also** *Tsebaoth***)—the Lord of Hosts.** The word *sabaoth* is *tsebaah* according to *Strong's Concordance* and is the word for "a mass," "a mass of people or things, such as an army." It is used to refer to a host of angels or heavenly bodies, a celestial army, or to all that the earth contains.

130. The name *Jehovah-Sabaoth* is not used in Scripture until the Book of 1 Samuel; following that, it is used in two out of three instances by individuals. At that time Israel did not apparently see her need to call upon God as Lord of Hosts. Yet when we read the prophets Isaiah, Jeremiah, Amos, Haggai, Zechariah, and Malachi, we find this name for God used over and over again. It appears fifty-two times in Zechariah's fourteen chapters, and eighty-three times in Jeremiah's fifty-two chapters.

131. God is repeatedly referred to as the Lord of Hosts in the Books of Isaiah and Jeremiah but not in Ezekiel. Why? Because this name belongs to a certain stage in the experience of God's people. This is a name for those who in the midst of a struggle find their own resources inadequate. In desperation they called on the name of *Jehovah-Sabaoth*. On the other hand, it is not a name used by those who have ceased to fight—such as those found in Ezekiel in the days when they were forced to settle into seventy years of captivity.

132. From God's perspective, Lord of Hosts is a name that reminds his people exactly who he is. Not only is he the one who delivers, he is also the one who judges. We see God in the Book of Malachi reminding his people over and over again of his name, *Jehovah-Sabaoth*. "'I am not pleased with you,' says the LORD of hosts. . . . 'For My name will be great among the nations,' says the LORD of hosts. . . . 'I am a great King,' says the LORD of hosts, 'and My name is feared among the nations'" (Mal. 1:10–11, 14 NASB).

133. *Jehovah-Shalom*—the Lord Is Peace. In the dark hours of Israel's history during the time of the judges, God revealed himself as *Jehovah-Shalom*, "the Lord is peace." The sons of Israel had done evil in the sight of the Lord, and he had given them into the hands of the Midianites for seven years. Things were bad for God's chosen people (Judg. 6:6). Midian prevailed against Israel, forcing them into mountain caves and dens. Judges 6 describes the Midianites coming up with the Amalekites to ravage and devastate the Israelites' crops and all their livestock. God's people were desperate for peace.

134. *Jehovah-Shalom* revealed true peace to Gideon. "When Gideon saw that he was the angel of the LORD, he said, 'Alas O Lord GOD! For now I have seen the angel of the LORD face to face.' The LORD said to him, 'Peace to you, do not fear; you shall not die.' Then Gideon built an altar there to the LORD and named it The LORD is

Peace" (Judg. 6:22–24 NASB). True peace cannot be found in any other place than in right relationship with God.

135. The basic underlying meaning of the Hebrew word *shalom* is "a harmony of relationship or a reconciliation"; therefore, the word is most often translated "peace" (approximately 170 times). The first time *shalom* appears in the Bible is in connection with "eternal peace." "Thou shalt go to thy fathers in peace" (Gen. 15:15).

136. The uniqueness of the word *shalom* **can be gathered from its alternative renderings:** "welfare" (Gen. 43:27); "good health" (Gen. 43:28); "all is well, safe" (2 Sam. 18:28–29); "prosperity" (Ps. 35:27); "favor" (Song of Sol. 8:10); "rest" (Ps. 38:3); "whole" (Deut. 27:6); "finished" (1 Kings 9:25; Dan. 5:26); "full" (Gen. 15:16); "make good" (Exod. 21:34); "restitution or repay, well or welfare" (Exod. 22: 5, 6); and "pay or perform in the sense of fulfilling or completing obligations" (Pss. 37:21; 50:14). Several times it is given as "perfect" (1 Chron. 29:19), the idea of wholeness or being in harmony with God.

THE GOD WHO IS THERE

137. *Jehovah-Shammah*—**the Lord Is There.** The children of Israel were in captivity and would be there for seventy years as a result of their sin (Jer. 29:10). They had heard from the prophet Ezekiel how the glory of the Lord had departed from the temple (Ezek. 10:18–19; 11:22–24). God had to judge his people for their adultery as a nation. "How I have been hurt by their adulterous hearts, which have turned away from me. . . . They will loathe themselves for the evil they have done. . . . And they will know that I am the LORD . . ." (Ezek. 6:9). God left them with a future hope.

138. *Jehovah-Shammah* **is found in the last verse** of the Book of Ezekiel where it is used in reference to the earthly Jerusalem, the city that the Lord Jesus Christ will inhabit when he returns to earth to reign as King of Kings and Lord of Lords. "The distance all around will be 18,000 cubits. And the name of the city from that time on will be: THE LORD IS THERE" (Ezek. 48:35).

139. The word *shammah* is simply the word for "there," but the fact that it is combined with Jehovah and the fact that the Spirit of God calls it a name makes it unique. When God named the futuristic city *Jehovah-Shammah,* he was assuring his people that he, Jehovah, would be there. It assured them of a future and gave them purpose.

140. God's presence did return to Jerusalem. Scripture tells us he came again to the temple when he was twelve, but although the Jews were impressed, they did not realize they were listening to *Jehovah-Shammah* (Luke 2:42–47). At the age of thirty, *Jehovah-Shammah* began his ministry among them (Luke 3:23). They saw his miracles and heard his words, but still they would not believe.

141. *Jehovah-Tsidqenu*—the Lord our righteousness. In a dark hour of judgment and failure, God revealed to his people another of his names—*Jehovah-Tsidqenu.* "This is the name by which he will be called: The LORD Our Righteousness" (Jer. 23:6). And with that revelation comes the promise of a new covenant, the covenant of grace and a new heart (Jer. 31:31–34; Matt. 26:26–28; Heb. 8:6–13).

142. To be right with God or to be *righteous* means to be "straight." It is more than goodness. It is to do what God says is right, to live according to his standards. To do so requires a new heart. "I will put my law in their minds and write it on their hearts. . . . For I will forgive their wickedness and will remember their sins no more" (Jer. 31:33–34). "I will give you a new heart and put a new spirit in you; I will remove from you your heart of stone and give you a heart of flesh. And I will put my Spirit in you and move you to follow my decrees and be careful to keep my laws" (Ezek. 36:26–27).

143. The Hebrew term *Tsedeq* depicts a full weight or measure toward God in the spiritual sense, as contrasted to justice, which is represented as a woman holding a pair of balanced scales in her hand. (See Job 31:6; Ps. 62:9.) *Jehovah-Tsidqenu* is like a river flowing throughout the whole of Scripture. Appearing well over a thousand times in Scripture, this word is translated as "right, righteous," and also as "just, justify," and "declared innocent."

144. The message of righteousness can be found on almost every page of the Bible. It is the chain of truth opening out in depth and force to grab our attention, not only because of its messianic nature but because of personal, practical implications. God wanted his children to recognize that goodness and character were of greater value than the wealth, wisdom, and ways of the world.

145. *Jehovah-Makkeh*—the Lord Shall Smite Thee. "I will recompense thee according to thy ways and thine abominations that are in the midst of thee; and ye shall know that I am the LORD that smiteth *[Jehovah-Makkeh]*" (Ezek. 7:9 KJV). The American Standard Version translates the passage, "Ye shall know that I, Jehovah, do smite." God had dealt graciously with his people, but they had despised his grace. They refused to walk in his statutes and to keep his judgments. Because of the gross sin of the people, he had to deal with them in judgment.

146. *Jehovah-Gmolah*—the God of Recompense or Vengeance (he will fully repay). While *Jehovah-Gmolah* may withhold his judgment, vengeance is ultimately meted to those who mock his authority. The weeping prophet, Jeremiah, wrote: "Babylon has been a golden cup in the hand of the LORD [Jehovah], intoxicating all the earth. The nations have drunk of her wine; therefore the nations are going mad" (NASB). As a result, "the destroyer is coming against her, against Babylon, and her mighty men will be captured, their bows are shattered; for the LORD is a God of recompense, He will fully repay" (Jer. 51:7, 56 NASB).

147. Vengeance belongs to God, not to us. "Recompense to no man evil for evil. . . . Avenge not yourselves, but rather give place unto wrath: for it is written, Vengeance is mine; I will repay, saith the Lord" (Rom. 12:17–19 KJV). Solomon, whose name means peaceful, also gave us this advice, "Do not say, 'I'll pay you back for this wrong!' Wait for the LORD, and he will deliver you" (Prov. 20:22). Our nature says that people must be paid back their just due whether for evil or good. But God instructs us to leave the matter to him; he will right our cause and deal with those who treat us unjustly.

THE LORD OUR GOD

148. *Jehovah* versus *Adonai*. When *Lord* is in capital and small capital letters the word is *Jehovah;* otherwise the word is *Adonai* or *Adon*. When you read the Old Testament and see LORD, you are reading what in Hebrew is *YHWH, Jehovah*.

149. The name *Adonai* brings clarity to Christ's Sermon on the Mount. Jesus said, "Why do you call me, 'Lord, Lord,' and do not do what I say?" (Luke 6:46). "Not everyone who says to me, 'Lord, Lord,' will enter the kingdom of heaven, but only he who does the will of my Father who is in heaven" (Matt. 7:21–23). *Lord* is more than a word; it indicates a relationship. As this Scripture clearly indicates, the lordship of God means his total possession of us and our total submission to him as Lord and Master.

150. As *Adonai*, God has a right to expect obedience. This is why God became angry with Moses when he called him to go before Pharaoh and tell the ruler to let God's people go (Exod. 4:10–14). "Then Moses said to [Jehovah], 'Please, *[Adonai,]* I have never been eloquent, neither recently nor in time past, nor since You have spoken to Your servant; for I am slow of speech and slow of tongue.' . . . Then the anger of the LORD burned against Moses" (NASB). Why did God's anger burn? Because Moses was saying, "Lord, Lord *[Adonai]*," but not trusting or submitting to God as his Master.

151. Jesus as Lord *(Adonai)*—If God the Father is Lord, it is true also of God the Son. Jesus once asked the Pharisees, "'What do you think about the Christ? Whose son is he?' 'The son of David,' they replied. He said to them, 'How is it then that David, speaking by the Spirit, calls him "Lord"? For he says, "The Lord said to my Lord: 'Sit at my right hand until I put your enemies under your feet.'" If then David calls him "Lord," how can he be his son?' No one could say a word in reply, and from that day on no one dared to ask him any more questions" (Matt. 22:42–46).

152. Jesus claimed to be *Adon*. He quoted Psalm 110:1 to prove to the Pharisees that he was the Son of God. As Jesus quoted the psalm, he also established the fact that he was *Adon*. The verse reads in Hebrew, "Jehovah says to my *Adon.*" In this passage, David was speaking prophetically of Christ, the Messiah.

153. "Lord" is a title translated from two words in the New Testament. *Kyrios* means supreme in authority, or controller. This is the most common word used in reference to Jesus Christ. The other is *despotes,* which means an absolute ruler, like a despot. "You call me 'Teacher' and 'Lord,' and rightly so, for that is what I am" (John 13:13; see Rom. 10:8–10). "Lord" is the one-word definition of God's sovereignty.

4

His Attributes

154. Perfectly balanced, perfectly integrated. In his book *The Knowledge of the Holy*, A. W. Tozer points out that there is no conflict between God's attributes within himself. He is perfectly integrated in his being; he is whole. This is what peace is. All of the expressions of God's character are perfectly balanced and perfectly manifested. What we call peace is the perfect, balanced expression of character that flows from a true and secure recognition of who God is.

155. Omnipresence. The first of the three compound words using the Latin prefix *omni*, meaning "all," is connected to the word "presence," meaning God is everywhere at once. God is present in all his creation but is in no way limited by it. Whereas immensity emphasizes the transcendence of God in that he transcends all space and is not subject to the limitations of space, omnipresence has special reference to his presence within the universe (1 Kings 8:27; Ps. 139:7–10; Isa. 66:1; Jer. 23:23–24; Acts 7:48–50; 17:24; Rom. 10:6–8).

156. The omnipresence of God means two things. The doctrine of the omnipresence of God is both comforting and subduing. It is a source of comfort, because God, the ever-present one, is always available to help us (Deut. 4:7; Pss. 46:1; 145:18; Matt. 28:20). But it is equally a source of warning and restraint. No matter how much we may try, the sinner cannot escape from God. Neither distance nor darkness hides us (Ps. 139:7–10). "And there is no creature hidden from His sight, but all things are open and laid bare to the eyes of Him with whom we have to do" (Heb. 4:13 NASB).

157. Omniscience. God is infinite in knowledge. He knows himself and all other things perfectly, whether they be past, present, or future. He knows things immediately, simultaneously, exhaustively, and truly. Scripture declares that God's understanding is infinite (Ps. 147:5; Isa. 46:10), that nothing is hidden from him (Heb. 4:13), and that even the hairs on our head are numbered (Matt. 10:30).

158. God knows himself perfectly. No created being has complete and perfect knowledge of self other than God. The Father, the Son, and the Holy Spirit know each other perfectly. The Trinity alone has intimate knowledge of each other. Jesus said, "No one knows the Son except the Father, and no one knows the Father except the Son and those to whom the Son chooses to reveal him" (Matt. 11:27). Paul wrote, "No one knows the thoughts of God except the Spirit of God" (1 Cor. 2:11).

159. God determines and knows all things. This includes inanimate creation (Ps. 147:4), all the beasts (Ps. 8:7), humanity and all their works (Ps. 33:13–15; Prov. 5:21), men's thoughts and hearts (Ps. 139:1–4; Prov. 15:3), and men's burdens and wants (Exod. 3:7; Matt. 6:8, 32).

160. God orders all things into being. God knew that Keilah would betray David to Saul if David remained in that vicinity (1 Sam. 23:11–12). Jesus knew that Tyre and Sidon would have repented had they seen the miracles that were done in Bethsaida and Chorazin (Matt. 11:21). He also knew the cities of Sodom and Gomorrah would have been spared had they seen the works that were done in Capernaum (Matt. 11:23–24).

161. God knows the future. From humanity's standpoint, God's knowledge of the future is foreknowledge, but from God's standpoint it is not, because he knows all things by one simultaneous intuition. He foreknew the future in general (Isa. 46:9–13; Daniel 2, 7; Matthew 24–25; Acts 15:18), the sinful course that Israel would take (Deut. 31:20–21), the rise of Cyrus (Isa. 44:26–45:7), the coming of Christ (Micah 5:2), and his crucifixion at the hands of wicked men (Acts 2:23; 3:18).

162. Omnipotence. God is all-powerful and able to do whatever he wills. Since his will is aligned with his nature, God can do everything that is in harmony with his perfections. Some things God cannot do because they are contrary to his nature as God. He cannot look with favor on iniquity (Hab. 1:13), deny himself (2 Tim. 2:13), lie (Titus 1:2; Heb. 6:18), or tempt or be tempted to sin (James 1:13).

163. God's possession of omnipotence does not demand the exercise of his power, and certainly not the exercise of *all* his power. In other words, God has power over his power. Omnipotence includes the power of self-limitation. God has limited himself to some extent by giving free will to his rational creatures.

164. The Bible clearly teaches the omnipotence of God. The Lord, who is called "Almighty" (Gen. 17:1; Rev. 4:8), is said to be able to do all things he purposes (Job 42:2), for with him all things are possible (Matt. 19:26) and nothing is too difficult (Jer. 32:17). He indeed reigns (Rev. 19:6).

165. Absolute versus ordinate power. A distinction can be made between God's absolute power, meaning that God may work directly, and his ordinate power, meaning he often uses second causes for divine intervention. Absolute power is used in creation, miracles, immediate revelation, inspiration, and regeneration.

166. To the Christian, the omnipotence of God is a source of great comfort and hope. The believer is urged to trust God in every walk of life with the knowledge of his creative, preserving, and providential power (Isa. 45:11–13; 46:4; Jer. 32:16–44; Acts 4:24–31). On the other hand, to the unbeliever, a God so mighty should be a source of fear (1 Peter 4:17; 2 Peter 3:10–12; Rev. 19:15). Even the demons shudder (James 2:19), knowing that God has power over them (Matt. 8:29). Someday even the strongest and greatest will seek to hide from God (Rev. 6:15–17), and every knee will bow at the name of Jesus (Phil. 2:10).

167. God is immutable and unchanging. All change is either for better or worse, but God cannot change to the better, because he is absolutely perfect; neither can he change for the worse, for the same reason. He can never be wiser, more holy, more just, more merciful, more truthful, or less so. Neither do his plans and purposes change. Scripture declares that there is no variation with God (James 1:17). He does not change with regard to his character (Ps. 102:26–27; Mal. 3:6; Heb. 1:12), his power (Rom. 4:20–21), his plans or purposes (Ps. 33:11; Isa. 46:10), his promises (1 Kings 8:56; 2 Cor. 1:20), his love and mercy (Ps. 103:17), or his justice (Gen. 18:25; Isa. 28:17).

168. Immutability is not to be confused with immobility. God is active and enters into relationships with changing people. In these relationships it is necessary for an unchangeable God to alter his dealings with changing humanity in order to remain constant in his character and purposes. For example, God deals differently with people before salvation than after (Prov. 11:20; 12:12; 1 Peter 3:12), and when his children change from evil to good, or from good to evil (Gen. 6:6; Exod. 32:14; Jer. 18:7–11; Joel 2:13; Jonah 3:10). God's immutability consists in always doing right.

GOD'S MORAL ATTRIBUTES

169. The holiness of God. God is absolutely separate from and exalted above all his creation, and he is equally separate from all evil and sin. God is perfect in all that he is. God's will is always the expression of his nature, which is holy.

170. Holiness in the Old Testament. Holiness is the attribute by which God wanted to be known in the Old Testament times.

It is emphasized by the boundaries set on Mount Sinai when God came down upon it (Exod. 19:12–25)—the division of the tabernacle and temple into the holy and most holy places (Exod. 26:33; 1 Kings 6:16, 19), the prescribed offerings (Leviticus 1–7), the special priesthood to mediate between God and the people, the many laws about impurity, the feasts of Israel, and the special position of Israel in Palestine. The Lord is called "the Holy One" some thirty times in Isaiah alone.

171. Holiness in the New Testament. In New Testament times, holiness is ascribed to God with less frequency than in the Old, but is still prevalent (John 17:11; Heb. 12:10; 1 Peter 1:15.). The angels around the throne of God sing "Holy, holy, holy" (Isa. 6:3; Rev. 4:8). The holiness of God, rather than the love, the power, or the will of God, should be given first place. Holiness is the regulative principle of the other three, for his throne is established on the basis of his holiness.

172. Righteousness and justice. Righteousness and justice are the aspects of God's holiness that are seen in his dealings with his creation. Abraham pondered, "Will not the Judge of all the earth do right?" (Gen. 18:25). The psalmist declares, "Righteousness and justice are the foundation of your throne" (Ps. 89:14; 97:2). (See *Jehovah-Tsidqenu,* chap. 3, no. 141.)

173. The goodness of God. In the larger sense of the term, the goodness of God includes many qualities such as God's holiness, righteousness, and truth. But in the narrower sense, God's goodness focuses on his love, benevolence, mercy, and grace.

174. The love of God is not a mere emotional impulse but a rational and voluntary affection, having its ground in truth and holiness. It exercises free choice. This does not deny feeling, for true love involves feeling. The fact that God grieves over the sins of his people implies that he loves his people with much feeling (Isa. 63:9; Eph. 4:30).

175. "God is love," the Scriptures declare (1 John 4:8, 16; 2 Cor. 13:11). It is his very nature to love. He initiates love (1 John 4:10). The Father loves the Son (Matt. 3:17), and the Son loves the Father (John 14:31). God loves the world (John 3:16; Eph. 2:4), his ancient people Israel (Deut. 7:6–8, 13; Jer. 31:3), and his true children (John 14:23). He loves righteousness (Ps. 11:7) and justice (Isa. 61:8). The assurance of God's love is a source of comfort to the believer (Rom. 8:35–39).

176. The compassion of God. The Lamb of God turned his cheek to the smiters and pled clemency for his murderers—and we read of Jehovah: "The LORD is compassionate and gracious, slow to anger, abounding in love" (Ps. 103:8).

177. The benevolence of God. Because of his goodness, God deals bountifully, tenderly, and kindly with all his creatures. "The LORD is good to all and His mercies are over all His works. . . . The eyes of all look to You, and You give them their food in due time. You open Your hand and satisfy the desire of every living thing" (Ps. 145:9, 15–16 NASB). The benevolence of God is made known in his concern for the welfare of humanity and is suited to our needs and capacities (Job 38:41; Ps. 104:21). His benevolence is not restricted to believers, for "He causes his sun to rise on the evil and the good, and sends rain on the righteous and the unrighteous" (Matt. 5:45).

178. The mercy of God. God's mercy is his goodness shown to those who are *in misery or distress*. Compassion, pity, and lovingkindness are other terms in Scripture that communicate much the same thing. God is "rich in mercy" (Eph. 2:4) and "is full of compassion and mercy" (James 5:11). The term is often used in salutations and benedictions (Gal. 6:16; 1 Tim. 1:2; 2 Tim. 1:2; 2 John 3; Jude 2). Most important, God judges in mercy.

179. The grace of God. The grace of God is shown toward those who are *guilty.* Scripture speaks of "his glorious grace" (Eph. 1:6), "the incomparable riches of his grace" (Eph. 2:7), "abundant grace" (1 Peter 4:10), and "true grace" (1 Peter 5:12). The exercise of grace, like that of mercy, is optional with God.

180. Scriptures show the grace of God revealed to sinners through his long-suffering delay of the punishment of sin (Exod. 34:6; Rom. 2:4; 3:25; 1 Peter 3:20) and his showering of humanity with blessings instead of immediate judgment (Heb. 6:7). He made provision for our salvation (1 John 2:2), gave us the Word of God (Hosea 8:12), and made possible the convicting work of the Spirit (John 16:8–11) and common grace (Titus 2:11). God's special grace is also often mentioned in salutations and benedictions (1 Cor. 1:3; 16:23; Eph. 1:2; Phil. 1:2; Rev. 1:4; 22:21).

181. God is truth. The truth of God is not only the foundation of all religion but of all knowledge. God is the source of all truth. The conviction that the senses do not deceive, that consciousness is trustworthy, that things are what they appear to be, and that existence is not merely a dream rests ultimately upon the truth of God. Many like Pilate ask, "What is truth?" (John 18:38). Ultimate truth or reality is God.

182. Jesus affirmed God as "the only true God" (John 17:3). John wrote, "We are in him who is true" (1 John 5:20). His revelations of himself in nature, consciousness, and Scripture are true and trustworthy (Ps. 31:5; Heb. 6:17–18).

5

His Nature

183. The nature of God is generally described with the terms "essence" and "substance," meaning that which underlies all outward display—the reality itself, whether material or immaterial, the substratum of anything. To speak of God is to speak of an essence, a substance, not of a mere idea or the personification of an idea.

184. God has life. Science generally defines *life* as "having the powers of growth, reproduction or creation, and the ability to adapt or initiate change." In contrast to the pagan gods of other religions, God is alive. He hears, sees, feels, acts, and is a live being. "For as the Father has life in himself, so he has granted the Son to have life in himself" (John 5:26).

185. God has spirituality. God is invisible, without physical parts, and is therefore free from this world's limitations. John 4:24 tells us that "God is spirit," which opposes the false notion that everything in the world can be explained by material things or the laws of nature. He can make himself known to humanity, but he is in essence an invisible yet personal spirit.

186. Humanity was made in God's image, which means that humans are *personal* beings, have intellect, retain a sense of morality, and have the ability to *choose* between right and wrong.

187. Though it says in the Bible that no one can see God, some verses speak of God's "hands," and we also find the interesting story of Moses observing God's back as he walks by. Such expressions are *anthropomorphic,* describing an infinite God in human terms in order to help us better understand him.

188. God is personal. God has a personal existence, rather than being an impersonal force. He chooses people, reaches out to individuals, and develops relationships with them. Rather than the false notion of pantheism, which teaches that God is in everything and therefore has no distinct existence, our God has intellect, sensibility, and will. He chose to die personally on our behalf in order to restore our relationship with him.

189. God has personality. Psychology usually defines personality as "being self-conscious and having the powers of self-determination." God chose to create us, desires to know us, and explains himself to us in ways we can understand. All of these point to a God with personality.

190. God has names that reveal his nature. The name "I Am" reveals his own self-consciousness. The name "the Lord Will Provide" suggests his desire for personal provision. "The Lord Is Our Peace" reveals God's action on man's behalf. "The Lord Our Shepherd" demonstrates his personal guidance and goodness. And "the Lord of Hosts" reveals his headship over us.

191. God has emotions. If emotions help reveal the personhood of God, it should be noted that the Bible speaks of God grieving (Gen. 6:6), loving (Rev. 3:19), hating (Prov. 6:16), becoming angry

(1 Kings 11:9), and becoming jealous (Deut. 6:15). The fact that he possesses emotions reveals that he must be personal.

192. God is the Creator. The Book of Genesis says that God is the creator of all things. The fact that he simply spoke things into being means he has infinite power and chose to use it in a personal way by creating mankind. As the prophet Isaiah puts it in 45:18, "He created it not in vain" (KJV).

193. God is a God of order. A quick look at creation reveals that he balanced the land and the sea, designed the intricate workings of our bodies, and spoke mighty mountains into existence. Rather than the world being haphazard and a product of random sampling, creation reveals a God who has carefully planned and ordered all things.

194. God takes care of us. Not only does he provide for our immediate needs, he personally directs and controls the free actions of men so as to determine all things in accordance with his eternal purpose. As Wordsworth said, "God foresees evil deeds, but never forces them."

195. God has a hand in human history. As the preserver of all things, not just setting creation in motion but becoming actively involved with our lives, God sustains us and watches over us. Everything from the writing of Scripture to the resurrection of Jesus, to making sure *you* heard the Good News is evidence of his concern for our eternal destiny.

196. God is our Father. While this is largely a New Testament concept (the fatherhood of God could not be established until the appearing of his Son), it is clear that Christ's mission on earth was to make God known as "Father." Similarly, no one can experience God as Father except through the work of Jesus Christ, whose work on the cross makes us all brothers and sisters in the family of God.

197. God is unified. There is only one God, with one essence, existing in three persons. Though God has three distinct faces (the Father, Son, and Holy Spirit), he remains a single, uniform being. Many heresies have been battled over the course of history regarding this point.

198. God is one, according to Deuteronomy 6:4, which does not mean he has one personality, but that his three persons exist in one being. There is only one God, the maker and sustainer of all life.

199. God is triune. As stated in the Athanasian Creed, "We worship one God in trinity and trinity in unity, neither confounding the persons nor dividing the substance." The Trinity is three eternally interrelated, interexistent, inseparable persons within one being. He is one in being and substance, possessed of three personal distinctions revealed to us as the Father, the Son, and the Holy Spirit.

200. God is self-existent. He is absolutely independent of all else. As Christ says in John 5:26, "The Father has life in himself. . . ." The meaning is not that God *invented* himself but that he is self-sustaining and has been for all eternity.

201. God is eternal and is called "the Everlasting God" in Genesis 21:33 (KJV). He had no beginning and will have no end. The past, the present, and the future are equally known to him.

202. God is immutable. As an infinite being, he transcends all change. We can't add to him, increase his power, or watch him grow and change. His nature, attributes, and counsel are unchanging. "I the LORD do not change" (Malachi 3:6).

203. When the Bible says that God repents or changes (such as in Jonah 3:10 or Gen. 6:6), it doesn't mean that the Lord actually changed his *mind* . . . only that he changed his *method*. God remains the same in character, but as people change their attitude toward God, he in turn seems to change his attitude toward people. It's really the *people* who change!

204. God is omniscient. He has perfect and complete knowledge. In the words of John Calvin, "God knows Himself and all other things in one Eternal and most simple act." Or, as Paul put it, "Oh the depth of the riches of the wisdom and knowledge of God! How unsearchable his judgments, and his paths beyond tracing out!" (Rom. 11:33).

205. God knows all things, according to 1 John 3:20. He knows everything about the world—all actions throughout eternity, the entire plan of the ages, and each individual's part in it. "The eyes of the Lord are everywhere, keeping watch on the wicked and the good" (Prov. 15:3).

206. If God knows everything before it happens, why doesn't he stop evil from occurring? The point must be made that *he does!* The Bible refers to God as our protector and gives clear examples of God holding back evil. However, the fact that he knows everything before it occurs does not mean he is the *cause*. Sometimes in his wisdom he allows evil to take place as part of his divine plan.

207. God is omnipotent. His power is unlimited by anyone or anything outside himself. Nothing is too hard for him; he can bring anything to pass. As it says in Matthew 19:26, "With God all things are possible."

208. All nature is subject to God's control. He spoke light into being, calmed storms with his words, and raised the dead to life. Yet he will not do anything inconsistent with the nature of things—for example, he will not make past events to have not occurred. With the exception of miraculous events, God works *within* the realm of nature.

209. All human action is dependent on God's will and subject to divine control. When King Nebuchadnezzar became too proud, God compelled his humility (Dan. 4:19–37). When Jonah attempted to run away from God, the Lord arranged for him to repent. According to Daniel 4:35, "He does as he pleases with the powers of heaven and the peoples of the earth. No one can hold back his hand or say to him: 'What have you done?'"

210. Angels and demons are under divine control. As created beings, they have no power over God's people unless the Lord allows it (see Job 1:12; Luke 22:31–32; James 4:7; Rev. 20:2).

211. God is omnipresent. He is active everywhere, not meaning that he is there in bodily form, but that his personal, spiritual presence is present everywhere at all times. "Where can I go from your Spirit? Where can I flee from your presence?" asked the psalmist David. "If I go up to the heavens, you are there; if I make my bed in the depths, you are there. If I rise on the wings of the dawn, if

I settle on the far side of the sea, even there your hand will guide me, your right hand will hold me fast" (Ps. 139:7–10).

212. God is particularly manifest in heaven. He is not necessarily "everywhere" in the same sense. His throne and his dwelling place are in glory.

213. God is holy. The angels seen by the prophet Isaiah tell us he is "holy, holy, holy," which is his most emphasized characteristic. We are told in 1 John that "God is love," but we're never told he is "love, love, love." God is holy—Isaiah tells us his very *name* is holy.

214. God is separate from all evil. "Be holy, because I am holy," he says in Leviticus 11:44. He is perfect in character, he hates sin, and he desires for his followers to be holy. He delights in all that is righteous.

215. God is righteous and just. His holiness is revealed in the fact that he recognizes our sinful condition and offers atonement on our behalf. The holiness of God magnifies his redeeming love, which provides a means of escape to those who are dead in their sins.

216. The justice of God is evident in the fact that he punishes wickedness and rewards righteousness. Yet his justice is tempered by his love—forgiving the sins of repentant believers and delivering his people from eternal death.

217. God is love. He always seeks the highest good for us and desires a close relationship with each individual. He gave himself up for us through his substitutionary death on the cross. "This is love: not that we loved God, but that he loved us and sent his Son" (1 John 4:10).

218. The object of God's love is, first of all, his own Son, and second, all humankind. God loves each individual. He loves the world—even the worst sinner in it. As it says in John 3:16, "For God so loved the world that he gave his one and only Son, that whoever believes in him shall not perish but have eternal life."

219. God's love is shown through his sacrifice on the cross. The amazing part of Christ's death is not simply that he died for those who love him, but that he also died for those who *hate* him!

Jesus even died for those who were putting him to death, revealing a love with no boundaries.

220. God is merciful. The word translated "mercy" means, literally, "lovingkindness." While mercy in the Old Testament generally had a negative connotation (lightening the misery of the guilty), the New Testament gave it the more positive meaning of being nicer to someone than he or she truly deserves.

221. God is gracious. Unique from mercy, the word *grace* retains the meaning of unmerited favor. The Lord grants humankind his favor as a gift. Salvation is not something we can ever earn or demand—it comes only by God's grace.

222. The purpose of God is to create life, allow it to fall, provide a means of salvation, and thus demonstrate his grace and greatness. From eternity God has purposed to save those people who believe in him, making them the object of his favor.

6

What God
Really Said

223. "God helps those who help themselves." This quote is
in fact from Benjamin Franklin, despite the fact that most people
assume it comes from the Book of Proverbs. The words were made
famous by President John F. Kennedy when he used them in one
of his speeches.

224. "A land flowing with milk and honey" were the words
God used to describe Palestine to Moses in Exodus 3:8. They are
now generally used to describe a fine or pleasant place.

225. "An eye for an eye" first appears in Leviticus 24:20. Rather than being a vindictive call for revenge, it actually limited the damage one person could do to another when taking retribution. Human nature encourages an individual to hurt others, but the Old Testament Law wanted to limit that hurt to equivalent damage.

226. "With God all things are possible." After explaining to the disciples how it would be easier for a camel to go through the eye of a needle than for a rich man to enter heaven, the disciples were understandably disillusioned with the concept of *anyone* getting into heaven. Jesus assured them that though it would be futile with men in charge, with God it was certainly possible to enter heaven (Matt. 19:25–26).

227. "The faith to move mountains." Although not currently used quite as often as it was in the twentieth century, the phrase refers to the power of belief. Jesus used this expression in Matthew 17:20 when talking to his disciples about healing the sick and the demon possessed.

228. "What God hath joined together . . ." Jesus spoke these words when he talked of marriage being a permanent covenant in Mark 10:9 (KJV). The words remain an important part of the traditional marriage ceremony even today.

229. "The salt of the earth." Many of the expressions we use in our culture come from the Lord Jesus. In describing his disciples with these words in Matthew 5:13, Christ emphasized their value—salt being the preferred method of payment in those days. The phrase is still used to describe people we find valuable or important.

230. "Holier than thou." God condemned those who considered themselves more self-righteous than their counterparts when he spoke against this attitude in Isaiah 65:2–5 (KJV). God mocked those who took such a position.

231. "Seek and ye shall find." These oft-quoted words of Jesus come from his Sermon on the Mount in Matthew 7:7 (KJV). It is still generally used as advice or encouragement to those who need to be seeking God's purpose and direction.

232. "The blind leading the blind . . ." Jesus spoke of false teachers when he used this expression. His point was that those teachers who are blind (do not know the real truth) cannot lead others anywhere that followers would want to go. Both the teacher and the followers will be lost and "fall into a ditch" as the verse goes on to say (Matt. 15:14 KJV).

233. "The spirit is willing, but the flesh is weak." Jesus spoke these words to his disciples the night of his betrayal. The disciples had fallen asleep after Jesus asked them to keep watch and pray with him. What is less quoted are the words Jesus quoted to the disciples before this phrase: "Watch and pray, that ye enter not into temptation" (Matt. 26:41 KJV). These words remind us why good intentions often lose out to weaknesses. Clearly Jesus suggested prayer and watchfulness to combat our weak flesh.

234. "The wolf in sheep's clothing." Jesus used this concept to describe false prophets who came to the people appearing as true teachers. He said, "Inwardly they are ferocious wolves" (Matt. 7:15), meaning that they were hypocrites and meant to lead people out of the safe "pasture" and into dangerous territory theologically.

235. "Cleanness of body was ever deemed to proceed from a due reverence to God," Francis Bacon (1561–1626) stated in his personal writings. Though Bacon might have wished it to be from the Bible, it is, in fact, not stated anywhere in that Book. From it many people have quoted, although the most popular version would be by John Wesley.

236. "Cleanliness is next to godliness." Stated by Wesley in 1772, the phrase "Certainly this is a duty, not a sin" preceded this now-famous quote. Though this might be a nice thought, it is hardly a biblical one and did not come from God.

237. "Do not throw pearls before swine." Jesus' words in Matthew 7:6 urge believers to take care with their message; it is not necessary to teach to those who are openly hostile to the gospel. A person wouldn't throw precious pearls to pigs, and Christians shouldn't throw the gift of salvation to those who will only turn around and attack them.

238. "Eat, drink, and be merry" was a phrase spoken by Jesus in Luke 12 while telling a cautionary tale about a rich fool thinking the rest of his life was set. The fool died that very night. The words are still generally used in a sarcastic or pejorative sense.

239. "The straight and narrow." Following the small, less traveled path leads to the narrow gate of life. In Matthew 7:14, Jesus cautioned people against following the more glamorous, broad, and well-traveled path that led to a wide gate full of destruction.

240. "The apple of my eye" is a phrase first used in Deuteronomy 32:10 to describe God's perspective of Israel. The Hebrew words literally mean "center" or "pupil" of the eye, but in the poetic sense the expression refers to someone or something highly valued by another. The poet David asks God in Psalm 17:8 to "keep me as the apple of your eye."

7

Surprising Symbols

241. Why symbols? One reason the Bible abounds in symbols is that it was written in the East where language was picturesque and people saw mirrors of spiritual truths in natural objects. Another more obvious reason may be that God, because of his infinity, had to express himself in speech that finite minds can understand in order to make clear and plain his being, revelation, and purpose.

242. Ancient of Days. Daniel repeats this name of grandeur three times to stress the importance of his vision (Dan. 7:9, 13, 22). His narrative describes a central throne shaped like a chariot with wheels as burning fire upon which the Judge sat, whose name was the "Ancient of Days." The prophet had been outlining the nature of four succeeding empires and then presents Jehovah in contrast to earthly kings—not only as enduring, but as Judge of the whole world. The Hebrew word used here for *ancient* means "advanced in age." Literally, the phrase "Ancient of Days" implies "a very old man"—the attribute of age expressing the majestic figure of the Judge. "God . . . abideth of old" (Ps. 55:19 KJV).

243. Ezekiel saw on a throne "the likeness as the appearance of a man" (1:26 KJV). This same prophet refers to "ancients of the house of Israel" (8:12 KJV; see also Jer. 19:1). Above the fleeting phases of life sits one who remains eternally the same (Pss. 90:1–3; 102:24–27). Hair as white and pure as wool symbolizes its owner as one who is holy and revered, and coincides with John's vision of the glorified Jesus whose head and hair was "white like wool, as white as snow" (Rev. 1:14).

244. Dazzling white raiment and beautiful white hair suggest the eternal being before whom an innumerable host stands in awe and adoration. These are characteristics of Christ, "the same yesterday, today, and forever." When Christ the Son of man appears crowned and with a sickle to reap the harvest of earth, he is depicted as one sitting on a cloud, and in this character he bears the attributes and moral glories of the Ancient of Days (Dan. 7:13; Rev. 1:13–14; 14:14).

245. The sun. God is the source of light and life. No more graphic symbol is used in Scripture to illustrate all that God is in himself. "For Jehovah God is a sun" (Ps. 84:11 ASV). "The sun of righteousness shall rise, with healing in its wings" (Mal. 4:2 RSV). If it were not for the sun, all the world would perish in darkness. Just as the natural sun is king of the planets; its creator is king over all humanity. Without his provision of heat and light, we could not exist.

246. Crown and diadem—God in his sovereignty and radiance. Isaiah says that "Jehovah of hosts *(Jehovah-Sabaoth)*" shall become "a crown of glory, and a diadem of beauty" unto the remnant of his people (28:5 ASV). Jehovah is known for his luster and loveliness. "How great is His beauty" (Zech. 9:17 KJV). A "crown of glory" is fitting for him who is the "King of Glory," and whose righteousness is "glorious" (2 Cor. 3:9–11). Truly he is incomparable! The wonder is that he waits to make us the recipients of all that he is in himself. Jesus prayed that his God-given glory might adorn our lives (John 17:22).

247. Wall of fire. The prophet Zechariah gives us the most forceful symbol of our God: "For I, saith the LORD, will be unto her a wall of fire round about, and will be the glory in the midst of her" (2:5 KJV). A "wall" is frequently used in Scripture as being symbolic of protective forces around us. Here the prophet presents the Lord as a "wall of fire" around his own. Many trials and tribulations threatened to overtake the children of Israel between the days of Zechariah and the coming of Christ. Even while Jerusalem is hemmed in on every side by enemies, God has not forgotten his promise to shield Jerusalem. With the surrounding fire of God's presence comes the promise "No weapon that is formed against thee shall prosper" (Isa. 54:17 KJV).

248. Refiner, purifier. "He will sit as a refiner and purifier of silver" (3:3), says Malachi of God's sanctifying work. God takes his time to make us holy. Patiently he sits at the crucible of our lives and separates out all that is alien to his holy mind and will. Note the double process of a silversmith. First, he is the *refiner,* tempering the heat so that all the impurities in the silver are forced to surface. Second, the refiner becomes the *purifier* as he skims the surface and removes all the dross. When does the silversmith know when his silver is thoroughly refined and purified? When he can see his own reflection on the surface.

249. The Rock. Symbols in Scripture were written by those who lived in Eastern lands, and they described God in terms of what was most familiar to them. Mountains surrounded Jerusalem with refreshing shade and shelter, offering travelers relief from the scorching heat of the desert sun. Prophets and psalmists, then, familiar with the protection of rocks, would know God as their Rock more so than Westerners.

250. An ancient Hebrew legend states that God had two bags of rocks when he made the world. He scattered the contents of one bag over the entire earth—but all the other rocks in the other bag he dropped on the small area of the Holy Land.

251. The Rock reveals God in his strength and stability. The original word for *rock* is also translated as "strength." "O LORD my strength" (Ps. 19:14 KJV). The Old Testament frequently refers to rock as a symbol of God's strength and stability. The psalmists especially loved this metaphor for God: "He is my Rock" (Ps. 92:15). This figure of speech reveals God in his permanence and unchangeable character.

252. Rock of Ages. Isaiah describes God as "the Rock eternal" (26:4). As Moses rebuked Israel for her idolatry, he spoke these words, "Of the Rock that begat thee thou are unmindful, and hast forgotten God that formed thee" (Deut. 32:18 KJV). In fact, in this chapter Moses speaks of the Rock four times:

- "The Rock of his salvation" (32:15 KJV)—the source of grace
- "The Rock that begat thee" (32:18 KJV)—the source of life
- "Their Rock had sold them" (32:30)—the source of ownership
- "Their rock is not like our Rock" (32:31)—the source of perfection

253. Cover/canopy—God as our protector and comforter. In 2 Kings 16:18, King Ahaz removed the "covert" (KJV) or "the covered way"(ASV). Opinions differ on the word's meaning. But possible explanations include a gallery belonging to the temple, the place where the king stood or sat during the Sabbath services, a public place for teaching, or the way by which the priest entered the sanctuary on the Sabbath. The word itself, from which we take *cover* or *canopy,* means a shelter of any kind (Isa. 4:6). It is used as a hiding place (Job 38:40); a place of secrecy (1 Sam. 25:20; Isa. 16:4); a den, or lair (Jer. 25:38). Applied to God, the symbol is a comforting picture of his protection and loving care of those who rest in his presence, "I long to . . . take refuge in the shelter of your wings" (Ps. 61:4).

254. City of Refuge—God is our haven from the enemy. The original Hebrew words for *refuge* are translated: "high tower," "shelter," and "hope" (Pss. 9:9 ASV; 61:3 KJV; Jer. 17:17 KJV). "The eternal God is thy refuge, and underneath are the everlasting arms" (Deut. 33:27 KJV). This promise emphasizes a double safety for the saints. Not only is the everlasting God our refuge, but his everlasting arms are around us.

255. Refuge. The first reference to *refuge* in Scripture is in connection with the "six cities of refuge" that Joshua set up as places of asylum to protect those who had shed blood accidentally. These asylums of safety were appointed by God (Isa. 26:1). At every crossroad on the east and west of Jordan was marked an appointed protection (Isa. 30:21). "Then the LORD said to Moses: '. . . "When you cross the Jordan into Canaan, select some towns to be your cities of refuge, to which a person who has killed someone accidentally may flee"'" (Num. 35:9–11). Likewise God is our only safety from the avenger. In him we are secure from the judgment of the law.

256. Fortress—God as our defense against the foe. "Jehovah is my . . . fortress" (Ps. 18:2 ASV). In times of war and conflict, the image of a fortress, often high up and inaccessible, provided perfect safety from enemies and persecutors. The names *Strong Tower* and *High Tower* as applied to God express a similar provision and purpose (Pss. 61:3; 144:2). Some thirteen times in the Psalms, God is exalted as our fortress or high tower. The writer exults in the protecting care and power of God: "I will love thee, O LORD, my strength. The LORD is my rock, and my fortress, . . . my high tower" (Ps. 18:1–2).

257. The shield is the most ancient and universal weapon of defense and was made in two varieties. The large shield, worn by heavily armed artillery, adapted to the form of the human body. It was made in an oval shape or in the shape of a door, hence the Greek name for *shield*, meaning "a door." Then there was the light, round buckler, like those the men of Benjamin carried (2 Chron. 14:8). The two kinds are often mentioned together (Ps. 35:2; Ezek. 23:24). Solomon boasted of having two hundred shields of beaten gold, and three hundred bucklers of beaten gold made to hang in the forest house at Lebanon (1 Kings 10:16–17).

258. Shield of faith. While instructing us to put on the whole armor of God, Paul spoke of faith as the large Greek-Roman shield, able to quench the fiery darts of hellish forces. A shield not only warded off sword thrusts or objects hurled at it but actually stood between the soldier and his foe. God is the preserver and protector of his children; our shield stands between the enemy and ourselves.

259. Husband. First, God is our maker. "All things were made by him." But Jehovah is also a husband. Hosea depicts Israel as the wife of Jehovah and illustrates her unfaithfulness as she went after other lovers. God is shown as the divine husband striving to win back his faithless wife by wooing her back from all her evil wanderings. Yet there is another side of God's role of husband spoken through Jeremiah: "Leave thy fatherless children, I will preserve them alive; and let thy widows trust in me" (49:11 KJV).

260. Governor. As we consider the worn, torn condition of our world today, it does not appear that God is ruling as its governor. Yet in the present tense, the psalmist writes about him who "doeth according to his will among the inhabitants of the earth." "For the kingdom is the LORD's: and he is the governor [ASV gives "ruler"] among the nations" (Ps. 22:28 KJV). The term *governor,* from the original meaning "to rule," is the same word used for Joseph whom Pharaoh appointed governor over all Egypt (Gen. 42:6). God alone is the perfect governor. He alone holds the divine right to govern the nations.

261. Redeemer. The word *redeem* first appears in Scripture in connection with Jacob's blessing of his son Joseph, where the verb is written in the present tense, "The angel who has redeemed me from all evil" (Gen. 48:16 NASB). *Goel,* the Hebrew term for "redeem," came to be used as the nearest blood relative, whose duty it was to avenge a murder. Jacob, however, used it in a broader sense as a deliverer or savior (see Exod. 6:6; Isa. 59:20).

262. "Redemption" implies freedom and an entire change of state or condition and therefore differs from "purchase," which describes a simple exchange of owners. Though a slave may be purchased, it does not necessarily mean he or she is delivered from slavery. When God speaks of his redemption of Israel, however, he makes possible both a change of masters *and* condition. "In your unfailing love you will lead the people you have redeemed" (Exod. 15:13).

263. King. Kings and kingdoms dominate the Bible as is seen by the fact that the term *king* occurs some 2,400 times, and *kingdom* some 350 times. Fascinated by the pomp and splendor of surrounding kings with their courts and palaces, Israel became dissatisfied with serving and obeying an invisible deity. She wanted a visible, authoritative human king to lead her (1 Sam. 8:6). The Israelites' request (or demand) meant that the people had not actually rejected Samuel, who acted as God's representative, but as Jehovah said, "They have rejected me as their king" (1 Sam. 8:7).

264. "Earthly kings come and go, but God is 'an everlasting king'" (Jer. 10:10). He is "the King eternal, immortal, invisible, the only God," worthy of "honor and glory for ever and ever. Amen" (1 Tim. 1:17).

265. A symbol of Christ in the Old Testament. God said to Moses, "Thou shalt smite the rock, and there shall come water out of it, that the people may drink" (Exod. 17:6 KJV). At the cross, the Rock of Ages was smitten, and at Pentecost, water flowed out of it through the giving of the Holy Spirit (1 Cor. 10:4).

SALT, OIL, AND WINE

266. Salt. Ancient Hebrews had an unlimited supply of salt. They formed brine pits called "salt-pans" along the Dead Sea's flat coastal area. The sun evaporated the water in the pits, leaving behind an abundant supply of mineral salts. Salt was the chief economic product of the ancient world, and the Hebrews used it in a variety of ways: for flavoring foods, preserving fish, curing meat, and pickling olives and vegetables.

267. Jesus used salt to give flavor and preserve other substances (Matt. 5:13; Mark 9:50). All who have accepted the Holy Spirit through salvation are to be used by him to preserve the earth from corruption, to season its blandness, to heal, and to freshen. We are the salt of the earth because of the Spirit's indwelling.

268. Salt for seasoning/flavor. From ancient times, salt has been recognized as one of the most important elements in the seasoning of food. Job was asked by Eliphaz, "Is tasteless food eaten without salt?" (Job 6:6). May even our "conversation be always full of grace, seasoned with salt" (Col. 4:6). The role of the Holy Spirit within our lives is to keep the gospel message savory.

269. Salt for healing. In Bible lands, infants were rubbed with salt to ensure good health before swaddling. And salt was believed to have been an antidote for tooth decay. Salt was an ingredient in the sacred anointing oil and ritual sacrifices symbolizing God's perpetual covenant with Israel (Num. 18:19). Salt purifies as does the work of the Holy Spirit. Here it serves as a symbol for inner healing as well as physical healing.

270. Salt for preservation. Without refrigeration, people of ancient Bible lands relied on salt to preserve their meats from rotting. Likewise all who are born again by the Holy Spirit are to be used by him to preserve the earth from corruption. We are the salt of the earth, because the Holy Spirit dwelling in us is holy.

271. Oil was a main item in every Jewish household. The olive, native only to the lands bordering the Mediterranean Sea, was the most important tree cultivated in the Holy Land. A single large olive tree in biblical times provided an entire family with all of the oil it needed—as much as half a ton a year.

272. The use of oil for anointing is beautifully symbolic of the manifold ministry of the Holy Spirit. Many accounts of anointing are presented in the Bible, each carrying different meanings of the custom as a way of showing courtesy, respect, even devotion; for healing purposes; and as a symbol of the pouring out of God's Spirit. "God anointed Jesus of Nazareth with the Holy Spirit and power" that he might do good and heal all those under the power of evil (Acts 10:38).

273. Oil for healing. "Is any one of you sick? He should call the elders of the church to pray over him and anoint him with oil in the name of the Lord" (James 5:14). Oil not only acts as a healing agent for the body, it also symbolizes the quiet work of the Spirit who alone can heal our bruised hearts.

274. Oil for illumination. Jesus called his disciples "lights," or lamps. The indwelling Spirit as oil enabled them to shine and maintain an effective witness in dark days. Light comes from within, as does spiritual illumination made possible by the Spirit. This is not to be confused with what men call "the light of reason," which can keep them in darkness as far as spiritual truth is concerned (see Ps. 119:105).

275. Wine. When the Holy Spirit came at Pentecost, a crowd gathered, and some made fun of the apostles, thinking they were drunk. But Peter stood up and addressed the crowd saying, "These men are not drunk, as you suppose. It's only nine in the morning!" (Acts 2:15). Such was the effect of the Holy Spirit. Their spiritual exhilaration and joy and their amazing display of linguistic power was mistaken for drunkenness. "Do not get drunk on wine. . . . Instead, be filled with the Spirit" (Eph. 5:18). The more deeply and repeatedly we drink of him, the more capacity we have and the more we will desire.

276. Seed (1 John 3:9). In the fullness of time, Jesus came as the seed of a woman—the seed implanted within her by the Holy Spirit when he overshadowed her, making her the mother of our Lord (Luke 1:31, 35): "to thy seed, which is Christ" (Gal. 3:16 KJV). The Scripture, which reveals him, is also likened unto a seed (Luke 8:5). Peter calls it imperishable seed (1 Peter 1:23).

277. Seal. Like his Master, Jesus, Paul knew how to use what was around him to illustrate divine truth. His numerous military metaphors, for example, reflect his long and close association with the Roman army. While at Ephesus, a prosperous maritime city in the apostle's day, Paul came to know of its extensive timber trade and noticed that when the great logs and planks were brought in and sold, they were then sealed with burnt-in marks indicating ownership.

278. A seal for the completion of a transaction. Under ancient Jewish law, when an agreement was completed and the price paid, a seal was applied to the contract to make it definite and binding (Jer. 32:9–10). The moment a person is reborn in the Spirit, he or she is sealed with the Spirit, and because he is the Seal, he cannot be broken. With this Seal, we are no longer our own. We now have the divine stamp upon us, which marks us as divine property until the day of final redemption (Rom. 8:23).

279. A seal communicated the image of its originator. In ages past, an imprinted design of a seal would be pressed into melted wax (such as a monogram or recognized symbol) and often implied a finished transaction when applied to documents. It is said of Jesus, "him hath God the Father sealed" (John 6:27 KJV), and he was "the express image of his person" (Heb. 1:3 KJV), just as the wax bore the image of the seal.

280. Earnest or deposit (2 Cor. 1:22; 5:5; Eph. 1:13–14). *Earnest* generally means a deposit paid by a purchaser to give validity to a contract. Paul used the symbol in this sense: "Who hath . . . given the earnest of the Spirit in our hearts" (2 Cor. 1:22 KJV). The Spirit is our pledge, the deposit on our complete inheritance. The symbol of the earnest, relative to the Holy Spirit, is used by Paul three times in connection with the believer's redemption-inheritance.

281. Our English word *earnest*. "*Arrabon,* originally meant earnest—money deposited by the purchaser and forfeited if the purchase was not complete, and was probably a Phoenician word, introduced into Greece. In general, the word came to mean a pledge of any sort. In the New Testament it is used only of that which is assured by God to believers: It is said that the Holy Spirit is the Divine pledge of all their future blessedness, particularly of their eternal inheritance. (See Gen. 38:17, 20, 25.) In modern Greek, *Arrabona* is an engagement ring."—W. E. Vine

282. Clothing. The phrase "came upon" literally means, "the Spirit of Jehovah clothed himself with Gideon" (Judg. 6:34 ASV margin). Clothing as a verb is frequently used in a figurative sense (see Isa. 61:10). *Endued* implies "clothed with power from on high" (Luke 24:49). The Spirit's empowerment is likened to an act of clothing or covering. Often the Spirit cast himself like a mantle around those he sought to use for a specific purpose. Acting in free sovereignty, he came upon men. "He came upon [clothed himself with] Gideon" (Judg. 6:34). "He came upon [clothed himself with] Amasai" (1 Chron. 12:18). "He came upon [clothed himself with] Zechariah" (2 Chron. 24:20).

283. Some symbols are drawn from natural life. What a perfect reflection of the spiritual is the natural! How gracious of God it is to convey heavenly truth through the media of natural elements we are accustomed to. In this way infinity enlightens our finite understanding. The emblems used to convey the Spirit's attributes and activities are as windows allowing light to reach our minds so that we can more readily understand the things of the Spirit.

284. Wind. In the original text, *spirit* means wind or breath. That the Holy Spirit is the secret of all life and vitality is evident from this forceful symbol describing his activity. As the natural wind is air in motion, so in the spiritual realm, the Spirit is God in action.

285. Breath. Just as God breathed upon Adam and he became a living soul (Gen. 2:7), the new creation in Christ is birthed by the breath of the Holy Spirit. "And with that he [Jesus] breathed on them and said, 'Receive the Holy Spirit'"(John 20:22). Job emphasizes this same truth in the phrase, "The breath [wind] of the Almighty . . . gives him understanding" (Job 32:8; see also 33:4). In his prophecy of Israel, Ezekiel also prayed to the Spirit, "Come from the four winds, O breath, and breathe into these slain, that they may live" (37:9).

286. Just as the wind is invisible, unpredictable, and out of human control, yet powerful in its effects, it is a fitting symbol of the mysterious work of the Holy Spirit. While speaking to Nicodemus, Jesus said, "The wind blows wherever it pleases. You hear its sound, but you cannot tell where it comes from or where it is going. So it is with everyone born of the Spirit" (John 3:8).

287. The wind's forces. At times wind comes with hurricane force, yet it can become as soft as a whisper upon one's cheek. The hard, cruel jailer in the Book of Acts needed the Spirit's power in great magnitude (Acts 16:25–31). But no cyclone experience was necessary for Lydia, whose heart silently opened to the Lord in Acts 16:14.

288. A mighty wind. Luke describes the coming of the Spirit on the Day of Pentecost "as of a rushing mighty wind" (Acts 2:2 KJV). *Rushing* suggests the irresistible action of the Spirit and *mighty* speaks of power. The Spirit who came to impart power to witness (Acts 1:8) is all powerful in himself (Micah 3:8).

289. Acting as a sudden and mighty wind, the Spirit can control and do as he deems best with those he desires to use. "God's ways are as mysterious as the pathway of the wind [Spirit]," says Solomon (Eccles. 11:5 TLB). "The Wind of God," the Spirit is often found in vehement action, as is illustrated in the following passages:

- "The Spirit lifted me up between earth and heaven" (Ezek. 8:3).
- "Then the Spirit lifted me up and brought me to the gate of the house of the LORD" (Ezek. 11:1).
- "Then the Spirit of the LORD came upon me" (Ezek. 11:5).
- "The Spirit of the Lord caught away Philip . . . was found at Azotus" (Acts 8:39–40 ASV).

290. Water is one of the most common symbols used to describe not only the varied ministry of the Holy Spirit but also the Holy Scriptures. The symbol of water is easy to understand and was used in several passages of Scripture for cleansing (Ezek. 36:25–27); life, fertility, beauty (Ezek. 47:1–12); and joy (Isa. 12:3). We could not live without water or rain. "Whoever drinks the water I give him will never thirst" (John 4:14).

291. Living Water. Clean water is one of the necessities of life, and in his conversation with the woman at the well, Jesus sought to show her how the Holy Spirit, as a well of water within her, provided not only clean water but Living Water. He was her only source of spiritual life and refreshment. As Living Water, the presence of the Spirit in the heart quenches thirst and produces life. He alone satisfies the soul's deepest thirst.

292. Rivers or streams. Rivers or "streams of living water. . . . By this he meant the Spirit, whom those who believed in him were later to receive" (John 7:37–39). Written in plural form—rivers, streams—our Lord's prophecy indicates the variety and abundance of the Spirit's activities. Consider the diversity of his dealings with us. Many rivers and streams cover the earth, yet no two are alike.

293. Floods. Just as water flooded the earth with judgment in Noah's day, a deluge of the Spirit is just as able to engulf the earth with blessing. The flood not only symbolized destruction, but it can stand for the lavish and bountiful supply of the Spirit.

294. Rain. "May he come down like rain" (Ps. 72:6 NASB). Absence of rain means famine, scarcity, and ruin as many arid countries experience. The church is certainly suffering from spiritual famine and is in need of the abundance of rain. May he send upon her the latter rains of the Spirit for he alone can transform the desert, causing it to blossom as the rose (Isa. 35:1; Joel 2:23).

295. Springs. "Indeed, the water I give him will become in him a spring of water welling up to eternal life" (John 4:14). Springs are not only reservoirs of pure, fresh water, but the *source* of great rivers. Said the psalmist, "All my springs are in thee" (Ps. 87:7), and this is true of the Spirit, who is our "secret source of every precious thing." In Christ we have an unending source of supply—a Spring that never ceases to flow.

296. Dew. "I will be like the dew" (Hosea 14:5). The Anglican *Book of Common Prayer* has a request for "the continual dew of Thy blessing," and this is what the Spirit waits to bestow upon every believer. Shakespeare has a phrase about "morning roses newly washed with dew." Secretly, unnoticed through the night and early morning, the dew descends upon the earth. So also the Holy Spirit comes quietly and rests upon us.

297. The Spirit's fire (Isa. 4:4; Acts 2:3). Twice John the Baptist said of Jesus, "He will baptize you with the Holy Spirit and with fire" (Matt. 3:11; Luke 3:16). The Spirit is the fire, as symbolized when he came upon the disciples at Pentecost as "cloven tongues like as of fire" (Acts 2:3 KJV; see also Luke 12:49; Rev. 4:5). The symbol of fire is also used to portray the holy presence and character of God (Deut. 4:24; Heb. 12:29) and also of the Word itself (Jer. 5:14; 20:9; 23:29).

298. Fire consumes what is combustible and tests what is not. It cleanses that which neither air nor water can cleanse.

299. Fire gives light. As fire, the Spirit is the source of spiritual illumination and knowledge. He enlightens the eyes of our understanding (Eph. 1:17–18; Heb. 6:4).

300. Fire purifies. As fire, the Spirit exercises his power to purify, to judge and consume all impurity, and burn within us all that is not in conformity with his holy will (Lev. 10:2; Mal. 3:2–3).

301. Fire gives heat. "I am warm; I see the fire," said the writer of Isaiah (44:16). How quickly fire can warm—symbolizing the Spirit's power to shed God's love that warms cold hearts (Rom. 5:5).

Fire gives life and warmth. Somehow the church at Ephesus had lost this warmth (Rev. 2:4).

302. Fire gives power. In the life and service of the believer, the Holy Spirit is a driving power. He is the fire in the boiler, the energizing influence in our witness (see Lev. 9:24; 10:2; Acts 2:3–4).

303. "Came mightily upon." Akin to clothing is the strong verbiage about the Spirit who "came mightily upon" certain leaders. Literally the phrase implies that he attacked men, and as a greater force, compelled those he arrested to accomplish his task. As the Omnipotent One, he "came mightily upon" Samson (Judg. 14:6, 19; 15:14 KJV), "came mightily upon [Saul]" (1 Sam. 10:6, 10 ASV), and "came mightily upon David" (1 Sam. 16:13 ASV).

304. "Upon." Further, there is the softer, milder term *upon,* expressing a temporary divine covering. Many illustrations of this action of the Spirit can be found in Scripture (e.g., Num. 11:17; 24:2; 1 Sam. 19:20, 23; Isa. 59:21; 60:1). Another gentle term is that of *rest,* used in connection with the mantling of the Spirit, and is associated with his dovelike character. The Spirit "rested on" the seventy elders (Num. 11:25–26), rested upon Elisha (2 Kings 2:15), and rested upon the Messiah (Isa. 11:2).

305. Seven. Representing perfection, the number seven is symbolic of the Holy Spirit in the perfection of deity, and also in the perfection of his mission. He is spoken of as having:

- "seven eyes" (Zech. 3:9; 4:10; Rev. 5:6), symbolizing possession of perfect insight, knowledge, and understanding.
- "seven horns" (Rev. 5:6). Horns symbolize power, and the Spirit is perfect in power and authority.
- "seven spirits" (Rev. 1:4). We see here perfection of manifestation, as well as perfect obedience to the divine will.
- "seven lamps of fire" (Rev. 1:12–13). Symbolic of divine holiness, these lamps suggest the Spirit's holiness.

306. As the sevenfold Spirit, he is intimately associated with the seven churches, and is revealed as having a separate message and ministry for each of the churches (Revelation 2–3).

307. A dove represents the Spirit's gentleness, tenderness, peace, beauty, innocence, patience, and sincerity. When Jesus was initiated into his public ministry, "the Holy Spirit descended on him in bodily form like a dove" (Luke 3:22). Such semblance proclaimed two things, namely, the Spirit's own nature and the loving, quiet, gentle, mission Jesus was to undertake—one of sacrifice. Six characteristics of the dove given in the Bible are applicable to the Spirit.

* Swift in flight—wings like a dove (Ps. 55:6)
* Beautiful—wings of a dove covered with silver (Ps. 68:13)
* Constant in love—the eyes of doves (Song of Sol. 5:12)
* Mournful—mourn like doves (Isa. 59:11)
* Gentle—harmless as doves (Matt. 10:16)
* Particular—"The dove found no rest for the sole of her foot" (Gen. 8:9 KJV).

308. Porter/doorkeeper. Scripture is rich in many direct, evident, and unmistakable symbols of God the Father, God the Son, and God the Holy Spirit. There are also *implied* symbols. The occupation of the porter is one of these implied designations of the Spirit. The Greek word our Lord used for porter was *thyroros,* the one who opens doors. Some scholars believe the porter Jesus spoke of was a reference to John the Baptist, who as Christ's forerunner came opening the door of the ministry of Jesus, or in other words, prepared his way (Mark 1:1–8). The Holy Spirit, however, was the divine forerunner of Jesus, and opened the door for his entrance into the world.

309. Paraclete/counselor. As a favorite designation for the Spirit, Christ used this symbol at least four times. As a paraclete, the Holy Spirit is an abiding counselor (John 14:16); he came as the gift of the Father (John 14:26); he is represented as the gift of the Son (John 15:26); and he came as Christ's gift at the time of ascension (John 16:7). Because the Greek language is pliable and gives one word several meanings, we have three words for *paraclete: comforter, advocate,* and *helper.*

310. Comforter. As such the Spirit is present and involved with our trials and sufferings. "Then the church throughout Judea, Galilee and Samaria enjoyed a time of peace. It was strengthened; and encouraged by the Holy Spirit" (Acts 9:31). The New American Standard Bible translates the rest of this verse "going on in the fear of the Lord and in the comfort of the Holy Spirit, it continued to increase."

311. Augustine once wrote, "The Holy Spirit on the Day of Pentecost descended into the temple of His Apostles, which He had prepared for Himself, as a shower of sanctification and a perpetual Comforter. . . . He is our sweetest Comforter."

312. Advocate/intercessor. "We have an advocate with the Father" (1 John 2:1 KJV). This term, which John applied to Jesus as our intercessor in heaven, and which Jesus himself used while on earth (Luke 22:31–32), is the same word translated "paraclete." It is a term representing a pleader who comes forward in favor of, and as the representative of, another. This idea is present in our two advocates. The Holy Spirit advocates, Christ pleads his cause for the believer (Rom. 8:26–27), and in heaven Christ intercedes for the believer (Heb. 7:25).

313. Helper. "In the same way, the Spirit helps us in our weakness" (Rom. 8:26). *Helper* is another word resident in the original "paraclete." Among the gifts of the Spirit is the help of the Helper himself. Paul obtained help from the Holy Spirit to continue his arduous labors (Acts 26:22). All believers can find in the Spirit the "grace to help us in our time of need" (Heb. 4:16).

314. Witness. Our Lord said of the Spirit, "He will testify about me" (John 15:26), and *testify* is the same word for *witness* in the original text. Throughout Scripture the Spirit is before us as a true and faithful witness for God the Father and the Son. Witness is related to an old English word, *witan,* meaning "to know." Paul proved the Holy Spirit to be a perfect witness in such passages as: "The Spirit Himself bears witness" (Rom. 8:16 NASB) and "My conscience bearing witness with me in the Holy Spirit" (Rom. 9:1 NRSV). As a witness, the Spirit's testimony is always in harmony with his own just and righteous nature. He witnesses in and to the believer in at least three ways: to our pardon, to our adoption, and to our sanctification.

315. Witness to our pardon. As sinners we are lost, and in the court of divine justice we are guilty of breaking the laws of God. But by pleading the saving grace of Jesus Christ, we are forgiven of our crime. The Spirit enters and stands as the witness of our divine pardon, assuring us that we are no longer under condemnation (Rom. 5:1; 8:1).

316. Witness to our adoption. The Holy Spirit witnesses with our spirits that we are the sons of God. From the court of justice, we have been pardoned and acquitted. We can now be adopted into the family of God. The Holy Spirit acts as our continued witness to our adoption as children and heirs of an eternal inheritance (Rom. 8:14–17; Gal. 4:6).

317. Witness to our sanctification. The indwelling Spirit is not only the evidence of our sonship, he is also the source of our holiness. Pardoned in court, we become children in the Father's house, and then holy ones serving in his temple. One reason why the Spirit is called holy is because it is his mission to empower us to live in holiness (2 Tim. 1:14).

318. Finger. Early church fathers spoke of the Holy Spirit as "the Finger of the Hand Divine." In Scripture, "the finger of God" and "the hand of God" are symbolic of his omnipotence and of divine authorship, visible in all God's works. The finger of God has five uses: as the Spirit of God, for writing the Law of God, as the judgment of God, as the power of God, and on the saints of God.

319. Finger—the Spirit of God. Combining what Matthew and Luke have to say about our Lord's miracle of casting out demons, we discover that the Holy Spirit is the finger of God: "I drive out demons by the Spirit of God" (Matt. 12:28). "I with the finger of God cast out devils" (Luke 11:20 KJV). "Finger," as Christ's title for the Spirit of Power, describes him accomplishing the purpose of God.

320. Finger—writing the Law of God. "Written with the finger of God" upon the two tablets of stone were etched the Ten Commandments (Exod. 31:18; Deut. 9:10). Jesus named the Spirit "the finger of God," hence the implication that he was associated with God in the framing and writing of divine truth. Also, while human fingers actually penned the Scriptures as a whole, they were under the direct control of the divine finger (2 Peter 1:21; 1 Peter 1:11).

321. Finger—the judgment of God. Two references to the divine finger are associated with judgment. First, when the magicians, in spite of their impressive enchantments, could no longer produce the same plagues with which God smote the Egyptians, they confessed to Pharaoh, "This is the finger of God" (Exod. 8:19). The second illustration of divine fingers being connected with judgment is found during the feast of Belshazzar, who shrank with fear as he saw "the fingers of a human hand" write out on the palace wall the drunken king's condemnation (Dan. 5:5, 24).

322. Finger—the power of God. Our first glimpse of the Spirit in Scripture is that of the Creator-Spirit (Gen. 1:2). David, a great lover of nature, considered the brilliant heavens God's masterpiece. He exclaimed, "O LORD, Our Lord, how majestic is your name in all the earth! . . . When I consider your heavens, the work of your fingers" (Ps. 8:1, 3a). The creative power of the Holy Spirit, the finger of God, still writes on the hearts of humanity as we are transformed into new creations in Christ Jesus (John 3:6–8; 2 Cor. 5:17; Gal. 6:15).

323. Finger—on the saints of God. To ancient Orientals, fingers were essential in conversation because they could indicate what their mouths dared not utter in respect to concern or grave insult. Referring to a wicked person who plots evil, Solomon wrote, "motions with his fingers" (Prov. 6:13). Isaiah also speaks of "the pointing finger and malicious talk" (Isa. 58:9). But Paul writes to the Corinthians in his second letter, reminding them that as a Christian church they were "a letter from Christ . . . written not with ink but with the Spirit of the living God" (2 Cor. 3:3). The Spirit writes upon the hearts of believers the laws of God (Heb. 8:10; 10:16).

324. Circumcision. God made a covenant with Abraham that brought with it a promise of unparalleled blessing. The sign of the covenant was circumcision. Every male of Abraham's descendants was to enter the covenant with the outward sign of circumcision. This rite was the key to releasing God's blessing to each subsequent generation, foreshadowing the "circumcision of the heart," when a person submits his or her life to the Lord Jesus Christ and receives the indwelling power of the Holy Spirit.

8

Famous Quotes

325. A philosopher once asked, "Where is God?" The Christian answered, "Let me first ask you, where is He not?"—John Arrowsmith

326. "The human mind, being created, has an understandable uneasiness about the Uncreated. We do not find it comfortable to allow for the presence of One who is wholly outside of the circle of our familiar knowledge. We tend to be disquieted by the thought of One who does not account to us for his being, who is responsible to no one, who is self-existent, self-dependent, and self-sufficient."—A. W. Tozer

327. "A sense of deity is inscribed on every heart."—John Calvin

328. "To say with all that we have, think, feel, and are 'God exists' is the most world-shattering statement that a human being can make. When we make that statement, all the distinctions between the intellectual, emotional, affective, and spiritual understanding fall away and there is only one truth left to acclaim: God exists."—Henri J. M. Nouwen

329. "The whole law of human existence lies in this: that man be able to bow down before the infinitely great."—Fyodor Dostoyevski

330. "Poetry is God's invitation to glimpse the unseen—His very character. The psalms were composed in poetic form, reaching beyond the world of sight and sound to reveal what our senses long to see and hear. In a voice that disrupts, invites, and reveals, the psalmist draws us to the voice of God."—Dan Allender and Tremper Longman

331. "Long, long before matter existed, before the cosmos took its first breath, before the first angel opened his eyes, when there was nothing—God had already lived forever. He had not just lived forever. He had been contented forever. And whatever God was, He still is and always will be."—Steven Estes

332. "God made man in his own image and man returned the compliment."—Blaise Pascal

333. "God so invested his image in our humanity that it is inescapably in operation. . . . We are pre-programmed to 'be,' to relate to other people, to comfort the grieving, to rescue the dying, and to reach out to touch the lonely and the sick. All of that is 'image of God' representation. And if we choose to save ourselves, to withdraw from the impulses to help, to rescue, to touch, then we are denying the image of God in us."—Donald and Robbie Joy

334. "The God of power, as he did ride/In his majestick robes of glorie / Resolv'd to light; and so one day / He did descend, undressing all the way."—George Herbert

335. **"If we cannot find God in your house or in mine,** upon the roadside or the margin of the sea; in the bursting seed or opening flower; in the day duty or the night musing; in the general laugh or the secret grief; in the procession of life, ever entering afresh, and solemnly passing by and dropping off; I do not think we should discern him any more on the grass of Eden, or beneath the moonlight of Gethsemane."—James Martineau

336. **"God is an utterable sigh,** planted in the depths of the soul."—Johann Paul Friedrich Richter

337. **"Joy is that deep settled confidence** that God is in control in every area of my life."—Paul Sailhamer

338. **"Omnipotence** which can lay its hand so heavily upon the world can also make its touch so light that the creature receives independence."—Søren Kierkegaard

339. **"Although power can force obedience,** only love can summon a response of love, which is the one thing God wants from us and the reason he created us. . . . Love has its own power, the only power ultimately capable of conquering the human heart."—Philip Yancey

340. **"God permits** what He hates to achieve what He loves." —Steven Estes

341. **"When I describe my children to people I meet,** I describe them by their attributes. These are words describing a quality or their inherent characteristics. For example, my older son Josh is creative and artistic. My daughter is dramatic, followed by her younger brother, the loud and boisterous adventurer. At first glance, these words can be confused with skills or abilities. But I use them to describe my children's inner nature. They have these qualities by nature and through the makeup of their character. As they age, these qualities will never change. God's attributes can be understood in the same way."—Doug Herman

342. **"'God is love,'** says the apostle John. 'Whoever lives in love lives in God, and God in him' (1 John 4:16). It would be difficult to get more personal than this."—Philip Yancey

343. "If God forgives us, we must forgive ourselves. Otherwise it is almost like setting up ourselves as a higher tribunal than him."—C. S. Lewis

344. "Once I 'know' God, that is, once I experience God's love as the love in which all my human experiences are anchored, I can only desire one thing: to be in that love."—Henri J. M. Nouwen

345. "The Holy Spirit is the bond of tenderness between the Father and the Son. Thus, the indwelling Spirit bears the indelible stamp of the compassion of God."—Brennan Manning

346. "The presence of God's glory is in heaven; the presence of his power on earth; the presence of his justice in hell; and the presence of his grace with his people. If he deny us his powerful presence, we fall into nothing; if he deny us his gracious presence, we fall into sin; if he deny us his merciful presence, we fall into hell."—John Mason

347. "The most costly sins I have committed came at a time when I briefly suspended my reverence for God. In such a moment I quietly (and insanely) concluded that God didn't care and most likely wouldn't intervene were I to risk the violation of one of His commandments."—Gordon MacDonald

348. "The first great commandment requires us to love God, which we do best through awareness of His great love for us. The 'remembering' of God, of which we sing in the Psalms, is simply the rediscovery, in deep compunction of heart, that God remembers us."—Thomas Merton

349. "Human language is at best insufficient to convey the full comprehension of the ideas of righteousness and justification contained in this word *[tsidqenu]*. It is only as we see it exhibited in God's character and acts that we see it clearly."—Dr. Nathan Stone

350. "The God who came to earth came not in a raging whirlwind nor in a devouring fire. Unimaginably, the Maker of all things shrank down, down, down, so small as to become an ovum, a single fertilized egg barely visible to the naked eye, an egg that would divide and redivide until a fetus took shape, enlarging cell by cell inside a nervous teenager."—Philip Yancey

351. **"Man's maker was made man** that He, Ruler of the stars, might nurse at His mother's breast; that the Bread might hunger, the Fountain thirst, the Light sleep, the Way be tired on its journey; that Truth might be accused of false witnesses, the Teacher be beaten with whips, the Foundation be suspended on wood; that Strength might grow weak; that the Healer might be wounded; that Life might die."—Augustine

352. **"My identity as Abba's child** is not an abstraction or a tap dance into religiosity. It is the core truth of my existence. Living in the wisdom of accepted tenderness profoundly affects my perception of reality, the way I respond to people and their life situations."—Brennan Manning

353. **"Joy is the most infallible sign** of the presence of God."—Léon Henri Marie Bloy

354. **"Were I a preacher,** I should preach above all other things the practice of the presence of God. Were I a teacher, I should advise all the world to it; so necessary do I think it, and so easy."—Brother Lawrence of the Resurrection

355. **"When, by the reception of the Holy Spirit,** I begin to realize that God knows all the deepest possibilities there are in me, knows all the eccentricities of my being, I find that the mystery of myself is solved by this besetting God."—Oswald Chambers

356. **"I have concluded** that the evident existence of God, and that my existence depends entirely on God in all the moments of my life, that I do not think that the human spirit may know anything with greater evidence and certitude."—René Descartes

357. **"Is God all-wise?** Then the darkest providences have meaning. We will set ourselves as God's interpreters, and because we cannot make straight lines out of our crooked lot, we think that God has turned our life into inextricable confusion. The darkest hours in our life have some intent, and it is really not needful that we should know all at once what that intent is. Let us keep within our own little sphere, and live a day at a time, and breathe a breath at a time,

and be content with one pulsation at a time, and interpretation will come when God pleases, and as he pleases."—Joseph Parker

358. "Prayer is essentially the expression of our heart longing for love. It is not so much the listing of our requests but the breathing of our own deepest request, to be united with God as fully as possible."—Jeffery D. Imbach

359. "'Repent and believe in the gospel,' Jesus says. Turn around and believe that the good news that we are loved is better than we ever dared hope, and that to believe in that good news, to live out of it and toward it, to be in love with that good news, is of all glad things in this world the gladdest thing of all."—Frederick Buechner

360. "After an exhaustive study was conducted on the great men and women of God throughout the centuries, one thing was found in common: They are marked by 'a holy leisure'—a sense of divinely ordered relaxation, an inner serenity that cultivates the wisdom to prioritize one's time and energy, and a productive leisure that kindles relationships and fires inspiration."—Gail MacDonald

361. "Love is giving someone else power to change. God knows that we can only change in the context of freedom. That is why he has lavished his favor on us: so that we could be cut free from every insecurity, healed of rejection's residue, and released from every sense of abandonment that would keep us from truly changing."—Steve Fry

362. "The first step to be taken by the soul who desires to draw near to God, is to learn to know God in very truth, and not only outwardly as though by the color of the writing. *For as we know, so do we love;* therefore if we know but little and darkly, if we reflect and meditate on Him only superficially and pleadingly, we shall in consequence love Him but little."—Angelina Foligna, a disciple of St. Francis of Assisi

363. "How can we pray to thee, thou holy and hidden God, whose ways are not our ways, who reignest in awful mystery beyond the realm of space and time? Yet how can we not pray to thee, Heavenly Father, who knowest what it is to be a man because thou hast walked among us as a man, breaking the bread of our affliction and drinking deep of the cup of our despair? How can we not pray to thee when it is thy very Spirit alive within us that moves our lips in prayer?"—Frederick Buechner

364. **"The Bible** sometimes portrays God as the initiator, yet just when we think we have God we suddenly feel like Isaiah searching for the One who absconds, *Deus absconditus.*"—Philip Yancey

365. **"The Bible knows** of God's hiding His face, of time when the contact between heaven and earth seems to be interrupted. God seems to withdraw himself utterly from the earth and no longer to participate in its existence. The space of history is then full of noise, but as it were, empty of divine breath."—Martin Buber

366. **"If you find God with great ease,** perhaps it is not God that you have found."—Thomas Merton

367. **"God is** like a person who clears his throat while hiding and so gives himself away."—Meister Eckhart

368. **"An 'impersonal God'**—well and good. A subjective God of beauty, truth and goodness, inside our own heads—better still. A formless life-force surging through us, a vast power which we can tap—best of all. But God Himself, alive, pulling at the other end of the cord, perhaps approaching at an infinite speed, the hunter, king, husband—that is quite another matter."—C. S. Lewis

369. **"The sensation of silence** cannot be helped: a loud and evident God would be a bully, an insecure tyrant, an all-crushing datum instead of, as He is, a bottomless encouragement to our faltering and frightened being."—John Updike

370. **"I envision the Spirit** not so much as touching our mundane lives with a supernatural wand as bringing the Recognition (Dorothy Sayer's word) of God's presence into places we may have overlooked. The Spirit may bring that jolt of Recognition to the most ordinary things: a baby's grin, snow falling on a frozen lake, a field of lavender in morning dew, a worship ritual that unexpectedly becomes more than ritual. Suddenly we see these momentary pleasures as gifts from God who is worthy of praise."—Philip Yancey

371. **"The soul must long for God** in order to be set aflame by God's love; but if the soul cannot yet feel this longing, then it must long for the longing. To long for the longing is also from God."—Meister Eckhart

372. **"We must flee to God** in our many tribulations whatever they may be—domestic worries, ill health, danger to those dear to us. The Christian can have no other refuge but his Saviour, his God. He will have not strength in himself, but in Him in whom he has taken refuge."—Augustine

373. **"'Joy,' said one of the martyrs, 'is the most infallible proof** of the presence of God.' . . . The presence of Jesus evokes a sense of joy. We will from time to time trust in the presence of Jesus. We will from time to time weep in the presence of Jesus. But when he is with us, and he always is, laughter will mark our lives. Joy is indeed the most infallible proof that his indwelling Spirit is in us."—Calvin Miller

374. **"How astonishing** that God chooses to give us a glimpse of Himself—however tarnished or imperfect the picture is to us— through allowing us to grapple with difficult emotions. As we seek a deeper grasp of our own emotions, the struggle opens our vision to see in fresh ways the heart of God."—Dan Allender

375. **"The reason** the mass of men fear God, and at the bottom dislike Him, is because they rather distrust His heart, and fancy Him all brain like a watch."—Herman Melville

376. **"Not many of us,** I think, would ever naturally say that we have known God. . . . We claim, perhaps, to have a testimony, and can rattle off our conversion story with the best of them; we say that we *know* God—this, after all, is what evangelicals are expected to say; but would it occur to us to say, without hesitation, that we *have known* God?"—J. I. Packer

377. **"God himself is present,** not in weakness that permits men to suffer without hope and perspective, but in the sovereignty of His love."—Karl Barth

378. **"There is only one question** which is really serious, and that is the question concerning the being and nature of God. From this all other questions derive their significance."—Emil Brunner

379. **"One can know a great deal** about godliness without much knowledge of God. There is no shortage of books on the church, or sermons from the pulpits, on how to pray, how to witness, how to read our Bibles, how to tithe our money, how to be a young Christian, how to be an old Christian, how to be a happy Christian, how to get consecrated, how to lead men to Christ, how to receive the baptism of the Holy Spirit (or, in some cases, how to avoid receiving it), how to speak in tongues (or, how to explain away Pentecostal manifestations), and generally how to go through all the various motions which the teachers in question associate with being a Christian believer . . . it is possible to learn a great deal at second-hand about the practice of Christianity. . . . Yet one can have all this and hardly know God at all."—J. I. Packer

380. **"That God is love** is certainly universally true, but it is not necessary truth, for He does not have to love us, nor does He owe it to Himself or to us to love us."—Thomas Torrance

381. **"Even the unbeliever encounters God,** but he does not penetrate through to the truth of God that is hidden from him."
—Karl Barth

382. **"They that deny** a God destroy man's nobility; for certainly man is of kin to the beasts in his body; and, if he be not of kin to God by his spirit, he is a base and ignoble creature."—Francis Bacon

383. **"Over time,** both through personal experience and my study of the Bible, I have come to know certain qualities of God. God's style often baffles me: He moves at a slow pace, prefers rebels and prodigals, restrains his power, and speaks in whispers and silence. Yet even in these qualities I see evidence of his longsuffering, mercy, and desire to woo rather than compel. When in doubt, I focus on Jesus, the most unfiltered revelation of God's own self."—Philip Yancey

384. **"The fact that God reveals Himself** through His Word presupposes that man is a being who has been created for this kind of communication, for communication through speech."—Emil Brunner

385. "Thou art the true, eternal, blessed, unchangeable light of all time and space. Thy wisdom apprehends thousands and still thousands of laws, and yet Thou ever actest of Thy free will, and to Thy honor. Thou wast before all that we worship. To Thee is due praise and adoration."—Ludwig van Beethoven

9

Prayers and Petitions

386. **"Prayer is the contact** of a living soul with God. In prayer, God stoops to kiss man, to bless man, and to aid in everything God can devise or man can need."—E. M. Bounds

387. **"The discussion of prayer** is so great that it requires the Father to reveal it, his firstborn Word to teach it, and the Spirit to enable us to think and speak rightly of so great a subject."—Origen

388. **"For everyone who asks receives;** he who seeks finds; and to him who knocks, the door will be opened" (Matt. 7:8).

389. **"In him and through faith in him** [Christ] we may approach God with freedom and confidence" (Eph. 3:12).

390. "**Oh highest heavenly Father,** pour into our hearts, through Thy son, Jesus Christ, such a light, that by it we may know what messenger we are bound to obey, so that with good conscience we may lay aside the burdens of others and serve Thee, eternal, heavenly Father with happy and joyful hearts."—Albrecht Dürer

391. "**My dear Lord,** only You I call and supplicate / About the vain and blind torment: / You only can renew me within and without."—Michelangelo Buonarroti

392. "**I obey Thee, Lord,** first for the love I, in all reason, owe Thee; secondly, because Thou can shorten or prolong the lives of men."—Leonardo daVinci

393. "**Lord!** That lends me life, lend me a heart replete with thankfulness."—William Shakespeare

394. "**Hear, O Israel:** The LORD is our God, the LORD alone [or, "the Lord our God is one"]. You shall love the LORD your God with all your heart, and with all your soul, and with all your might" (Deut. 6:4–5 NRSV). This is the Shema, the most commonly spoken prayer in Judaism, also traditionally called the "Great Commandment." Many Christians know it in the form that Jesus used in Mark 12:29.

395. "**May it be our lot,** by the grace of the true Son, pure and immaculate, to learn from Him, with all other truths, that which we are now seeking."—Galileo Galilei

396. "**For me, prayer means launching out of the heart towards God;** it means lifting up one's eyes, quite simply, to Heaven, a cry of grateful love from the crest of joy or the trough of despair; it is a vast, supernatural force which opens out my heart, and binds me close to Jesus."—Thérèse de Lisieux

397. "**Have mercy on me, O God,** according to your unfailing love; according to your great compassion blot out my transgressions. Wash away all my iniquity and cleanse me from my sin" (Ps. 51:1).

398. "**I thank the Lord Jesus Christ** . . . [and beseech him] to send me grace to bewail my guilts and to study to the salvation of my soul, and grant me grace of true repentance . . . through the benign grace of Him that is King of kings and Priest over all priests, that bought us with the precious blood of His heart."—Geoffrey Chaucer

399. "In the name of God, I William Shakespeare . . . God be praised, do make and ordain this, my last will and testament in manner and form following. That is to say, first I commend my soul into the hands of God my Creator, hoping and assuredly believing, through the only merits of Jesus Christ, my saviour, to be made partaker of eternal life, and my body to the earth whereof it is made."—William Shakespeare

400. "How easy it is for me to live with Thee Lord! How easy to believe in Thee! When my thoughts pull back in puzzlement or go soft, when the brightest people see no further than this evening and know not what to do tomorrow, Thou sendest down to me clear confidence that Thou art, and will make sure that not all the ways of the good are closed."—Aleksander Solzhenitsyn

401. "I tell you the truth, if anyone says to this mountain, 'Go, throw yourself into the sea,' and does not doubt in his heart but believes that what he says will happen, it will be done for him. Therefore I tell you, whatever you ask for in prayer, believe that you have received it, and it will be yours" (Mark 11:23–24).

402. "The house of my soul is too small for You to come to it. May it be enlarged by You. It is in ruins: restore it. In Your eyes it has offensive features. I admit it, I know it; but who will clean it up? Or to whom shall I cry other than You? 'Cleanse me from my secret faults, Lord, and spare Your servant from sins to which I am tempted by others' (Ps. 31:5)."—Augustine

403. "O people of Zion, who live in Jerusalem, you will weep no more. How gracious he will be when you cry for help! As soon as he hears, he will answer you" (Isa. 30:19).

404. "Father in heaven, now that another cloud the road / Effectively hides, and wrong ways I take / With uncertain walk among this unstable field / Of the worldly and marshy valley, / Sustain with Your holy hand, keep from failing / My erring way, and by Your mercy the light / Sweet over me shine, and for an escape / Show me the path that I had left behind."—Torquato Tasso

405. **"Oh God, God inconceivable** . . . I have erred . . . I knew that I was going astray . . . but I never forgot Thee. I always felt Thy presence even in the very moment of my sins. I all but lost Thee, but Thou hast . . . saved me!"—Leo Tolstoy

406. **"Let us pray for ourselves,** that we may not lose the word 'concern' out of our Christian vocabulary. Let us pray for our nation. Let us pray for those who have never known Jesus Christ and redeeming love, for moral forces everywhere, for our national leaders. Let prayer be our passion. Let prayer be our practice."—Robert E. Lee

407. **"O sad estate** / Of human wretchedness; so / weak is man, / So ignorant and blind, that / did not God / Sometimes withhold in mercy / what we ask / We should be ruined at our own request." —Hannah More

408. **"This, then, is how you should pray:** 'Our Father in heaven, hallowed be your name, your kingdom come, your will be done on earth as it is in heaven. Give us today our daily bread. Forgive us our debts, as we also have forgiven our debtors. And lead us not into temptation, but deliver us from the evil one'" (Matt. 6:9–13).

409. **"I am convinced** that when a Christian rightly prays the Lord's Prayer at any time . . . his praying is more than adequate." —Martin Luther

410. **"Come, Lord,** and speak to my heart. Communicate to it Your holy will, and mercifully work within it both to will and to do according to Your good pleasure."—Thomas à Kempis

411. **"God grant us the serenity** to accept the things we cannot change, the courage to change the things we can, and the wisdom to know the difference. Amen."—Reinhold Niebuhr

412. **"I ask you, Lord Jesus,** to develop in me, Your lover, an immeasurable urge towards You, an affection that is unbounded, a longing that is unrestrained, a fervor that throws discretion to the winds! The more worthwhile our love for You, all the more pressing does it become. Reason cannot hold it in check, fear does not make it tremble, wise judgment does not temper it."—Richard Rolle

413. "I do need Thee, Lord. I need Thee now. I know that I can do without many things that once I thought were necessities, but without Thee I cannot live, and I dare not die. . . . I ask of Thee no easy way, but just Thy grace that is sufficient for every need, so that no matter how hard the way, how challenging the hour, how dark the sky, I may be enabled to overcome. In Thy strength, who hast overcome the world, I make this prayer. Amen."—Peter Marshall

414. "Teach me, Lord, to sing of Your mercies. Turn my soul into a garden, where the flowers dance in the gentle breeze, praising You with their beauty. Let my soul be filled with beautiful virtues; let me be inspired by Your Holy Spirit; let me praise You always."—Teresa of Avila

415. "I have been driven many times to my knees by the overwhelming conviction that I had nowhere else to go. My own wisdom, and that of all about me seemed insufficient for the day."—Abraham Lincoln

416. "God be in my head, and in my understanding; God be in my eyes, and in my looking; God be in my mouth, and in my speaking; God be in my heart, and in my thinking; God be at my end, and at my departing."—Traditional Irish prayer

417. "Now I lay me down to sleep, I pray Thee, Lord, my soul to keep; if I should die before I wake, I pray thee Lord, my soul to take."—*New England Primer*

418. "Blessed are your saints, O Lord, who have traveled over the rough sea of this life, and have reached the harbor of eternal peace and joy. Watch over us who are still on the dangerous voyage. Our ship is frail, and the ocean is wide. But in Your mercy You have set us on Your course with Your son as our pilot, guiding us towards the everlasting shore of peace, the quiet haven of our hectic desire."—Augustine

419. "You, O Eternal Trinity, are a deep sea into which, the more I enter, the more I find, and the more I find, the more I seek. O abyss, O eternal Godhead, O sea profound, what more could You give me than Yourself? Amen."—Catherine of Siena

Part II

God's Story

10

The Creator

420. God began it all. "In the beginning God . . ." is how the first verse of the first chapter of the first book of the Bible begins. The beginning of the history of the world is chronicled with those words!

421. When creation began. Relying on biblical sources such as the chronologies and genealogies in Genesis, numerous people have attempted to pinpoint a time and date for the precise moment of creation. Ancient Hebrew scholars placed the moment at 3761 B.C. Perhaps the most famous creation date was the one produced by Irish bishop James Ussher (1581–1656). Using Genesis, Ussher dated the moment of creation to the early morning of the twenty-third of October in 4004 B.C. (Ussher actually used the Julian calendar year of 710). Ussher's calculation was widely accepted by European Christians for centuries and was included in the margins of many editions of the King James Bible, giving it nearly divine "authority."

422. Genesis 1:1 begins the summary of creation. "In the beginning God created the heavens and the earth." This first verse is considered a summary of what is to come in the following six days of creation (Gen. 1:3–31).

423. God's creation followed a specific order. Of the six days of creation, there is a parallel structure between God's creating work in days 1–3 and 4–6. The first segment of creation can be considered the forming of the structure of creation. The second segment includes the filling of that structure with every type of life.

424. On the first day, God created light. The light was separated from the darkness that had previously covered the earth. "Day" and "night" are introduced; the first day ends with "there was evening, and there was morning—the first day" (Gen. 1:5).

425. On the second day, God took a watery world and gave it definition. Whereas at the end of the first day, there was only water to see in the light, at the end of the second day there was sky present, separated from the waters.

426. On the third day, the waters under the sky were put in their place as dry ground appeared. God named the dry places "land" and the gathered waters "seas" (Gen. 1:9–10). The third day is also the first time when we read that "God saw that it was good" (v. 10).

427. During the second part of the third day, God made the land productive with fruit-producing trees and seed-bearing plants. Every imaginable seed-bearing plant and tree, every green living type of vegetation, was created at this time. God again stated that what he saw was "good."

428. On the fourth day, God began the second phase of his creation. Paralleling the creation of "light" and "day" from the first day, God creates two "great lights—the greater light to govern the day and the lesser light to govern the night" (Gen. 1:16). These great lights were put in the sky to serve as signs of the seasons as well as to separate the day from the night. The stars were also created on the fourth day. God again "saw that it was good" (v. 18).

429. On the fifth day, God filled the water and the air with every imaginable living creature. On the second day, he created the two expanses of sky and water; on this fifth day he filled those two portions of the earth. The "great creatures of the sea" and "every winged bird" were created, blessed, and given a command to increase their numbers. Showing his continuing pleasure with the creation, God saw it was good.

430. On the sixth day, God's creation had two parts. In the first part, God told the land to produce living creatures that will live on the land. This parallels the creation account of God creating "dry ground" on the third day. Also created on this day was man. God said, "Let us make man in our image, in our likeness" (v. 26). Man was told to rule over the living creatures in the sky, sea, and on the land. God told his two image-bearers (a male and a female) to increase their numbers too.

431. "Let us make man in our image . . ." Here God is speaking to those who are in heaven and watching what God is doing, his angels and the like. God mentions "us" again after the fall occurs, saying, "The man has now become like one of us, knowing good and evil" (3:22).

432. The second part of God's creative work on the sixth day involves what God gave man and the animals to live on. God gave man every "seed-bearing plant . . . and every tree that has fruit with seed in it" to eat (1:29). To every animal he gave the remaining vegetation—every green plant. This too parallels God's work on the third day; God had made vegetation during the latter half of the second day. On day six, he gave that vegetation over to his image-bearer and every living creature in order to eat and live.

433. Day six ends with God seeing everything he had done. On this final day, God saw that "it was very good" (v. 31). Chapter 2 opens with a final thought on the creation: "Thus the heavens and the earth were completed in all their vast array."

434. Eden, which means "a place of delight," is believed by some scholars to have been located at the eastern end of the Fertile

Crescent, near where the Tigris and Euphrates rivers meet the Persian Gulf.

435. The term *create* **is used in two senses in Scripture:** in the sense of immediate creation and in the sense of mediate creation. *Immediate* creation is that free act of the triune God in the beginning. Without the use of preexisting materials or secondary causes, he brought into being, immediately and instantaneously, the whole visible and invisible universe. *Mediate* creation, on the other hand, is those acts of God that are also called creation, but do not originate things. Instead they shape, adapt, combine, or transform existing materials.

436. Proof of creation. From ancient times humanity has been trying to solve the "riddle" of the universe. Humankind asks, "Did it always exist, or was there a beginning? If it did have a beginning, how and when did it come into being?" Science seeks to find an answer but is limited to empirical knowledge. Philosophy has not been able to arrive at an adequate solution either. The answer to our origin must ultimately come from Scripture and be accepted by faith (Heb. 11:3). Scripture declares both the how and why of physical and spiritual existence.

437. Creation was immediate, mediate, or a combination of both. Some limit immediate creation to the act described in Genesis 1:1 and regard the rest of the chapter as mediate creation. Others see a combination of both through the entire chapter. For example, the sun may have been included in the original creation, and the light (vv. 3–5) may have come from the sun. However, God most likely created light apart from the sun.

438. What was included in the immediate creation of God?
Certainly not only the heavens, but also the angelic inhabitants of heaven (Job 38:7; Neh. 9:6); and not only the earth, but also all the waters and gases of the earth (Isa. 42:5; Col. 1:16; Rev. 4:11).

439. The restoration theory, or "gap" theory, of creation proposes that after the original creation (Gen. 1:1), Satan fell, resulting in divine judgment upon the earth (v. 2). What follows are six days of recreating the earth. This view holds that "was" (v. 2) should be better translated "became." It further argues that the picture of formlessness, emptiness, and darkness (v. 2) is chiefly a picture of divine judgment, for God would not have created the earth this way (Isa. 34:11; 45:18; Jer. 4:23; 1 John 1:5). Further, this position provides a framework in which the fall of Satan may have taken place (Isa. 14:9–14; Ezek. 28:12–19).

440. Many philosophies deny the doctrine of creation and postulate other origins for the universe. Atheism, which denies the existence of God, must either make matter eternal or find some other natural cause. Dualism argues for two eternal principles, one good and one evil, or two eternal beings, God and Satan or God and matter. Pantheism makes creation a part of God. Agnosticism says no one can know about God or his creation.

441. Christianity affirms that creation came through God's sovereign will. God, though immanent in his creation, also transcends his creation. The universe is God's handiwork and is intended to display his glory.

442. The God of nature was once described by theologian J. I. Packer this way: "We are cruel to ourselves if we try to live in this world without knowing about the God whose world it is and who runs it. The world becomes a strange, mad, painful place, and life in it a disappointing and unpleasant business, for those who do not know about God. Disregard the study of God, and you sentence yourself to stumble and blunder through life blindfolded, as it were, with no sense of direction and no understanding of what surrounds you."

443. Adam and Eve were the first humans. We know God caused a deep sleep to fall upon Adam, and while he slept, God took one of Adam's ribs and closed up his flesh. Woman was then formed from the extracted rib. When the Old Testament was translated into Greek, the Hebrew word *tsela* in Genesis 2 became *pleura.* Only in its plural form does *pleura* refer to a set of ribs, but its more common translation is "side," "side of man," even the membranes that line the thoracic cavity. The term may even possibly refer to "wife," as the Hebrew *tsela* sometimes signifies a bosom friend or a person who is at one's side.

444. The word translated "rib" is not translated as such anywhere else in the Old Testament. Its most frequent use seems to be related to construction, and in references dealing with the building of the tabernacle, the word is translated "beam," "chamber," "plank," "corner," "sidechamber," and "side" (Exod. 25:12, 14; 26:27, 35; 27:7; 36:25–30).

445. God's sovereign rule. God, as creator of all things visible and invisible and the owner of all, has an absolute right to rule over all (Matt. 20:15; Rom. 9:20–21). He exercises his authority in the universe (Eph. 1:11). "Indeed everything that is in the heavens and the earth; Yours is the dominion, O LORD" (1 Chron. 29:11 NASB); "Woe to the one who quarrels with his Maker—an earthenware vessel among the vessels of earth! Will the clay say to the potter, 'What are you doing?' Or the thing you are making say, 'He has no hands'?" (Isa. 45:9 NASB); "Behold, all souls are mine; as the soul of the father, so also the soul of the son is mine" (Ezek. 18:4 KJV).

446. Humans were made in God's image, which means that we are *personal* beings, have intellect, retain a sense of morality, and have the ability to *choose* between right and wrong.

447. Genesis tells us that humans were created "in the image of God." This refers to the spirit and character which universally and unfailingly belong to humans only. Because God is spirit, we are created with the capacity for eternity and for valuing the self beyond our bodies.

448. *Imago Dei.* Only humanity is created in "the image of God." Though we share the same day of creation with all the animal kingdom and though we are made of the same stuff as the animals—the dust of the earth—only we are the *Imago Dei.*

449. Male or female? God is spirit and is therefore without body parts. Knowing that we, in our finite understanding, would need something tangible, God gave us symbols to bring us understanding of the great love offered to us. For example, the imagery of *parent—Father—*is one for us to grasp.

450. One flesh. The original "one flesh" union of the first man and woman forms a picture of the full spectrum "image of God." Differentiated as they were by the scalpel of God and formed into two distinct models—male and female—their first and almost involuntary response was to reach out and reattach to the other half, thus displaying God's personal and intimate nature.

451. God created them male and femaie *(Ish and Ishah)*.
In the creation of his most glorious reflection, the image of God is multifaceted, is specific and individual, but is also general and communal.

452. Adam and Eve's firstborn son, Cain, is remembered as the first murderer for killing his brother, Abel. When God sentenced Cain to wander the earth, Cain begged for mercy and, in fear, thought that someone would kill him. So God marked him. Widely viewed as a sign of guilt, the so-called mark of Cain is actually a symbol of divine mercy. Opponents of the death penalty point to this first murder and God's merciful sentence on the murderer as a biblical rejection of capital punishment. For his crime, Cain received a life sentence of hard labor.

11

His People

453. God's chosen people. One of the most significant lines in Amos is the prophet's message to Israel from God: "You only have I chosen of all the families of the earth; therefore I will punish you for all your sins" (3:2). This is the essence of the Jews' designation as the "chosen people." God's covenant with the people did not entitle them to special favors, but rather being chosen increased their responsibility.

454. Origin of the term "Jews." In the year 587 B.C., the holy city lay in ruins, and its people were led off to captivity in Babylon after the armies of King Nebuchadnezzar of Babylonia overran Judah and conquered Jerusalem. Their name changed to "Jews" (from the Hebrew *Yehudi,* which means "belonging to the tribe of

Judah"). They kept alive their faith and their way of life during their years of exile.

455. *Habiru* **(or "Hebrew")** was a word of disparagement, probably meaning "the dusty ones." It did not refer to the Hebrew people in particular but rather to all the land-hungry Semites who led a nomadic life. In the Book of Genesis (14:13), Abraham is called "the Hebrew," and so this general name was finally limited to his descendants.

456. The history of the Israelites. Through God's revelation of himself to the children of Israel, humanity first conceived of how they were originally created in the image of God, but fell from this high position after sinning. They learned of God's purpose of redemption through sacrifice, of deliverance through the death of a Messiah, of salvation for all nations, and of a final reign in righteousness and peace.

457. Abram was given his new name, Abraham, when God came to him in his ninety-ninth year. At that time he had one son, Ishmael. Abraham's new name meant "father of many nations." Abraham must have been puzzled how God would bring him into a full understanding of his new name with but one child when he was already quite old.

458. Throughout God's early conversations with Abraham, a covenant child was promised to continue this special man's line. God's promises are eternal; his words surpass logic and our plans of timing, and include a strong dose of miracles as well. Abraham and Sarah were unsure how this promise would come to be, as Sarah had been barren for many, many years. Though Abraham trusted God, he and Sarah also took matters into their own hands. Abraham made Sarah's maid, Hagar, pregnant, and though Abraham loved Ishmael and hoped God would make him the covenant son, God's will was already set. The Hebrews were told to trust God, to obey God, to follow him in all their ways, even when they didn't see exactly where that path was leading.

459. Abraham's covenant son, Isaac, was promised to Abraham first by God and then by the three angels who visited and prophesied of the event to Abraham shortly before Sarah discovered she was pregnant. Though Sarah laughed at their proclamation and

Abraham was undoubtedly skeptical, God's message carried his promise, something not to doubt. Sarah delivered a healthy infant son within a year of that proclamation, and they called this special baby Isaac. He was truly a miraculous sign of God's covenant with Abraham—Isaac's parents were in their nineties!

460. The sacrifice of Isaac. God called Abraham to follow him to a far land. God promised to make his family a great nation. Yet when Abraham finally had a son in his old age, the Lord asked him to sacrifice the boy on Mount Moriah. Instead of a pagan practice, it was a test of faith—God intervened to stop the sacrifice and provided a ram to sacrifice in the boy's place. Then, praising Abraham's faith, God promised to bless all nations through his offspring.

461. The story of Abraham's unshakable faith while offering Isaac is a central moment in the Bible. To many people it seems an unnecessarily cruel test of faith. Abraham doesn't even make the arguments for his own son that he made for the citizens of Sodom. His wife, Sarah, is silent in this episode, and Isaac's thoughts are not available to us either.

462. When God stays Abraham's hand. The passage says that Abraham "fears" God (Gen. 22:12). The "fear of God" is a commonly used expression today. The Hebrew verb for "fear" can be understood two ways. Occasionally it meant being afraid, but very often the biblical "fear" meant awe or reverence for someone of exalted position. Abraham was not necessarily "afraid" of God as much as he held God in profound respect.

463. Isaac was a godly patriarch and followed in his father's footsteps. He married Rebekah after Abraham sent Eliezer to find a wife for him. Eliezer's method of finding a wife was truly a testimony to his faith in God. Eliezer's prayer to God asked for a very specific sign to show him whom Isaac was to marry. He asked that the girl would be the one who, when Eliezer asked for water for himself, would say, "Drink, and I'll water your camels too." That very scenario occurred, and Eliezer confidently brought Rebekah to Isaac!

464. Isaac and Rebekah suffered some of the same difficulties as their parents—they were unable to have children too. It must have seemed impossible to imagine God's original covenant to Abraham of a people being greater "than the sands of the seashore" with both father and son being unable to have children on their own. Yet Isaac prayed to God for his wife, and she did become pregnant. Her twins represented two different nations; Jacob's family line would continue the covenant. Esau and Jacob were constantly at odds and only made peace many years after Jacob received the covenant blessing from his father, Isaac.

465. Jacob married two sisters, Rachel and Leah. Through deceit on the girls' father's part, Jacob was tricked on his wedding night. Jacob served Laban for seven years for Laban's younger daughter, Rachel. The morning after the wedding, Jacob found he had married Leah, Laban's older daughter, instead! Jacob agreed to serve Laban another seven years in exchange for Rachel.

466. Jacob was continually blessed. He experienced a dream early on that demonstrated God's faithful promise to be with him (Genesis 28). In addition to the blessing of his father, Isaac, God told him: "I will give you and your descendants the land on which you are lying. Your descendants will be like the dust of the earth, and you will spread out to the west and to the east, to the north and to the south. All peoples on earth will be blessed through you and your offspring. I am with you and will watch over you wherever you go" (vv. 13–15).

467. Wrestling with God. The life of Jacob contains a number of interesting stories that make him appear more a scoundrel than a patriarch. He cheated his brother, Esau, manipulated for a wife, and tricked his father. However, one of the strangest stories occurs in Genesis 32. While running from Esau, Jacob met God (appearing as a man) and wrestled with him all night. After having his hip torn from its socket, Jacob told the man that he would continue wrestling until he was blessed. With that God changed Jacob's name to *Israel*, which means, "wrestles with God."

468. Jacob had twelve sons by his two wives and their respective maids. These twelve sons would become the twelve seeds of the twelve tribes of Israel. The two sisters, Rachel and Leah, were bitter toward one another throughout their childbearing years. Rachel, Isaac's true love, could not produce children and was truly bitter toward Leah, who produced six sons. When God heard Jacob's pleas, as well as Rachel's, for children, God blessed them with the birth of a son, Joseph, and later Benjamin.

469. Joseph, though one of the youngest children of Jacob, was God's choice to continue his blessing. God consistently picked a son other than the firstborn and normal choice to be blessed and lead the family on. Joseph had many gifts, including the gift of interpreting dreams. He was continually blessed throughout his life.

470. The story of Joseph's "coat of many colors" remains a favorite of many people. His father gave him a special coat to wear that distinguished him from his brothers. Joseph was his father's favorite son, much to the chagrin of most of the other brothers. Jacob made Joseph his heir, even though he was the second to the youngest! Joseph's brothers eventually sold him into slavery in Egypt and joyfully took the coat, tore it up, and told Jacob his beloved son was dead.

471. God never forgot Joseph. Eventually this young man who saw visions and could interpret dreams made himself useful to Pharaoh! He became a chief minister of Egypt and was reunited with his family in their time of need during a drought spreading throughout the whole land. They all then settled in Egypt.

472. The twelve brothers and their father all remained in Egypt and lived happily there until the whole generation of Joseph and his brothers passed away. Then their people became oppressed by the Egyptians and were used as slaves. The Egyptians feared the great numbers of Hebrew people being born and even demanded that the midwives kill the newborn males. The oppression lasted over four hundred years!

473. Moses—or *Moshe* in Hebrew—is the central human figure in the Hebrew Bible, the great law bringer, and for Christians, the symbolic model for Jesus. God had a special plan for Moses. When the Egyptian pharaoh ordered all the Jewish babies killed, Moses was saved. His was a parallel experience to Jesus'—the Messiah was saved after a king ordered Jewish babies to be killed when Jesus was around two years old. His family ironically took the baby back to Egypt. Other instances of Moses foreshadowing Jesus: Moses parted the waters; Jesus walked on the waters. Moses spent forty years in the wilderness; Jesus spent forty days in the wilderness. Moses went to a mountain and gave a sermon; Jesus gave the Sermon on the Mount. Moses delivered the covenant; Jesus delivered the new covenant.

474. The escape from Egypt. Moses went before Pharaoh and demanded that his people be set free. The story of Moses, who was miraculously saved and raised as royalty, then lost his position due to immature violence only to be called by God to greatness, is a wonderful riches-to-rags-to-riches story. The plagues, the escape, and the parting of the Red Sea make it one of the most-told stories of all time.

475. The "Aaronic benediction" was given by God to Aaron, Moses' brother and the Israelites' priest. This extremely ancient blessing is still widely used in temples and churches today among both Jews and Christians: "The LORD bless you and keep you; the LORD make his face to shine upon you, and be gracious to you; the LORD lift up his countenance upon you, and give you peace" (Num. 6:24–26 NRSV).

476. God brought his people out of Egypt and they settled in the desert. The Israelites, as they had come to be called, didn't always trust God as they should have. They constantly forgot what a miracle their escape from Egypt was. Their disregard for this miracle led them to worship other gods and even to be angry at God. As a result, God put off taking them to Canaan until they had lived in the desert for forty years and a whole generation had died off.

477. Freed at last, the Israelites set about making a place in which to worship God. The tabernacle was their first place of worship. Very explicit instructions were given for how it was to be built (Exodus 26). Inside the tabernacle, which was a giant tent, were several rooms, including the Most Holy Place and the curtain separating that section from the Holy Place. The tabernacle was 75 feet by 150 feet in diameter.

478. The tent of the tabernacle was covered with badger skins. These skins are mentioned several times in the Old Testament. They were highly valued and listed along with gold, jewels, and other precious objects as materials for the tabernacle. Most badger pelts were extremely durable and tough, making excellent waterproofing for the tabernacle.

479. Some of the Israelites continued to disobey God in spite of the intensity of his miracles. Achan was one such case. During the battle of Jericho, he took some of the prized gold and other precious items that belonged to God and kept them for himself. As a result, the Israelites lost their next battle. God punished his people repeatedly for disobeying his commands, ever the faithful Father, yet a righteous God who demanded obedience.

480. Once the Israelites were established in Canaan, they were governed by judges, leaders who normally had first been warriors. God gave his people strong leaders to follow, but they didn't always do so. The Book of Judges tells of the difficulties the Israelites suffered when they did not obey God.

481. The ark of the covenant was the single most important object in the history of ancient Israel, though it eventually disappeared from the Bible without further mention. It was first housed in the tabernacle. It was a huge chest that contained the stone tables of the Ten Commandments. Above the chest hovered the wings of two cherubim. After Jerusalem was destroyed in 586 B.C. the fate of the ark was never discussed.

482. Saul was the first king of Israel. He was anointed by the prophet Samuel. Saul was known to be very tall and majestic of frame. God blessed Saul as long as he was obedient to God and listened to Samuel. But Saul fell away from God and suffered an unhappy ending. He became proud and jealous of David, a young man who was loyal to him and served him both personally and in battle. God did not allow Saul's sins to go unpunished. During a battle, Saul and many of his family were lost; Saul killed himself in order to avoid being captured.

483. David, the youngest son of Jesse, was anointed to be the second king of Israel when he was only a shepherd boy. He was a faithful witness to God's amazing love and found much joy and happiness as both a warrior and a king. Yet he too sinned and was punished. But he came back to God and was forgiven. David was also a famous poet—many of the Psalms were written by him.

484. Solomon became king in the year 961 B.C. and reigned for thirty-nine years. The name *Solomon* is derived from the Hebrew word for "peace," and Solomon indeed lived up to his name. Under Solomon's reign, Jerusalem became one of the most important cities in the Near East.

12

The Battle Belongs to the Lord

485. "If you [LORD] will deliver these people into our hands, we will totally destroy their cities" (Num. 21:2). Several Israelites were captured by the Canaanite king of Arad while the Israelites were traveling. God's people responded by making a vow to the Lord that they would destroy the cities if God would deliver the Canaanites into their hands. God listened to their plea and the Canaanites were defeated and their cities destroyed.

486. God remained the general of his people so long as the people deferred to him. When the two kings Sihon and Og opted to battle the Israelites rather than let them pass, God handed these forces into Israel's hands and allowed his people to kill everyone, capture their cities, and occupy their land.

487. At times God demanded vengeance of the Israelites, such as when they were ordered to attack the Midianites (Num. 31:1). Yet when God called his people to battle and they obeyed, they were blessed. At that particular battle, God delivered into Israel's hands the five kings of Midian as well as all their cities, flocks, people, and goods. Not a single Israelite fell in that battle!

488. The battle of Jericho is one of the most miraculous demonstrations of God's power to the Israelites as they became a new nation. The Israelites were instructed to march around Jericho one time each day for six days. The priests were to carry rams' horns at the front of the army. On the seventh day, the priests were instructed to blow the trumpets, then the people were all to shout. God promised Joshua that the walls would then collapse, and the men would be able to go inside the city walls and take the city. And it happened just as the angel promised Joshua it would.

489. The battle of Ai is a reminder of what happens when all Israel is not united in their obedience to the Lord. Achan, one of the Hebrew warriors, took for himself some of the plunder from Jericho instead of turning it all over to God. As a result, God did not give Ai into the Israelites' hands; instead, three thousand of their men were routed, some of them dying as a result of the disobedient Achan. God was angry with all Israel for this indiscretion, and his anger did not turn until Achan and all his household were destroyed. Again, God's actions are based on his complete righteousness. If the people obeyed, he blessed them. If not, he punished them.

490. God did eventually deliver Ai into the Israelites' hands. Joshua gave the soldiers strict orders on how to ambush the city. The Israelites were to pretend to flee as they had in the first battle; then their opponents would chase them. The battle worked out handily, with the entire city of Ai emptying out in order to chase the running Israelites. The city was left behind with no one to defend it. Some of the Israelite army then captured the city easily and set it on fire. The fleeing Israelites turned around to fight, with those in the city coming from behind. The Ai soldiers were struck down easily, and not one remained alive, not even their king. Then the Israelites took the livestock and plundered the city as God had instructed them to.

491. Enemies didn't stand a chance against the Israelites when the Lord was on their side! When the five kings of the Amorites joined forces against Israel, Joshua was assured by God that not a single one of their enemies would stand. God threw the Amorites into a confused state and made them flee. Then God pursued them by making big hailstones fall from the sky, an act that actually killed more Amorites than Israel did by the sword.

492. The sun stood still. While battling the Amorites, Joshua asked the Lord to allow the sun to stand in the sky until "the nation avenged itself on its enemies" (Josh. 10:12). The Bible account says that the "sun stopped in the middle of the sky and delayed going down about a full day. There has never been a day like it before or since, a day when the LORD listened to a man. Surely the LORD was fighting for Israel!" (Josh. 10:13–14).

493. "The LORD, the God of Israel, fought for Israel" (Josh. 10:42). Thanks to their God, the Israelites gained control of an entire region that had previously been ruled by peoples who were much stronger on a military front, had more riches and resources, and made alliances among others in their region. Yet those whom Israel defeated were idol worshipers, and they could not stand against God's power and righteousness. The Israelites left no survivors in their battles; they wiped out entire peoples as God had commanded them to.

494. Once the Southern region had been taken, the Northern kings became fearful and united in order to wage war on Israel. The Bible says they "came out with all their troops and a large number of horses and chariots—a huge army, as numerous as the sand on the seashore" (Josh. 11:4). God reminded Joshua that they were not to fear them, for he would hand over the entire lot to Israel. Joshua brought this message to the people and they attacked, without leaving a single survivor. The enemies' chariots were burned and their horses crippled.

495. Why were they warring? God had blessed his people with plenty of land and resources at this point, but the Israelites continued to battle. Why? God wanted the entire land taken as an inheritance for Israel; the Israelites didn't rest until they had done this. When they finished, they lived peacefully.

496. The time of the judges came after the death of Joshua. The judges were godly men and followed God. But after one judge would die, the people would revert to worshiping false gods and living as the people around them. Then God's anger would return, and the people would suffer oppression from those same people. All of the work of Joshua and his generation was undone in between the various judges. Many battles were lost in this time period as a result of Israel's disobedience.

497. Ehud was one such judge whom God used to deliver the people. The Moabites ruled over Israel for eighteen years before God allowed Ehud to deliver them. The Bible tells us Ehud was a left-handed man; this one characteristic is important to how the battle began. Ehud killed the king of Moab by tricking him. He met privately with the king and drew his sword from his right thigh with his left hand. He plunged it into the king and was able to get away without anyone even knowing what had happened. Afterward he sounded a trumpet and the other Israelites joined him to do battle against Moab. The Israelites won the battle and successfully ruled over Moab for eighty years.

498. The two most famous military heroines mentioned in the Old Testament are Deborah and Jael, judges who both had a hand in the same victory. God spoke through Deborah to tell the general Barak how to defeat the Canaanites, including their king, Jabin. Barak agreed to attack, but he wanted Deborah to go with him into the battle. She did and the enemies were defeated.

499. Gideon was called by God to "save Israel out of Midian's hand" (Judg. 6:14). At first Gideon led an army of thirty-two thousand men, but God told Gideon to send home all but three hundred! With trumpets, glass jars, torches, and faith in God's promise, the small Israelite army followed Gideon's lead and watched in amazement as they scared the Midianites awake. Then God caused the enemy soldiers to turn on one another with their swords before the whole bunch fled and were tracked down and killed.

500. During one particular battle, the ark of the covenant was taken by the Philistines. The Israelites were defeated on the battlefield and had lost four thousand of their men (1 Sam. 4:2). The people were fearful of why they had been defeated and requested that the ark be brought. When the Philistines realized that the Israelites' ark was in their midst, they descended on the Israelites' camp, killed thirty thousand more foot soldiers, and took the ark. This all happened in order to fulfill the prophecy of God given in 1 Samuel 2:30–35.

501. Samuel served as the last judge of the Israelites before Saul was made king. One particular battle demonstrated God's continuing faithfulness to Israel and involved this special judge. Samuel had assembled all the Israelites at Mizpah (1 Sam. 7:6–8). The Philistines heard that Israel was all in one place and hurried to wage war against them. Samuel took a lamb and offered it as a sacrifice to God and pleaded to him for his people. The Lord promised to take care of Israel, and he caused loud thunder to come around the Philistines, which caused them to panic. Israel then rushed in and pursued the Philistines, slaughtering them all.

502. Saul was the first king of the Israelites. The Lord worked in his heart and made him a true leader of the people. Before Saul was officially made king, yet after he had been anointed, God showed the people he was with Saul. The Ammonites besieged Jabesh Gilead, an Israelite stronghold, and the people were fearful and cried out for deliverance. They would not assemble to fight, however, choosing instead to send messages to the rest of Israel, asking for warriors to be delivered within seven days. When Saul heard about this plan, "the Spirit of God came upon him in power, and he burned with anger" (1 Sam. 11:6). He demanded that every able Israelite fight, and he raised 330,000 men total. They slaughtered the Ammonites and, as the Bible relays, "Those who survived were scattered, so that no two of them were left together" (1 Sam. 11:11).

503. Jonathan, the son of King Saul, also was successful in battle. He and his armor bearer climbed over a cliff to meet their Philistine enemies after Jonathan declared that "the LORD has given them [Philistines] into the hand of Israel" (1 Sam. 14:12). Together with his armor bearer, they killed twenty men in a space no larger than half an acre. Their attack spawned another attack after God caused a great panic among the Philistines. The enemy forces were so confused they were striking each other with their swords! Once again God demonstrated his faithfulness to Israel by winning the battle for them.

504. David fought Goliath because the Philistine giant had "defied the armies of the living God" (1 Sam. 17:36). David declared that God would deliver the Philistine into Israel's hands because God was with his people. With five smooth stones and only his sling as a weapon, the young shepherd boy defeated Goliath easily, assured that this was God's battle. Israel consistently found that if they trusted in God and sought his will, their enemies would not stand.

505. David lost favor with Saul and had to flee for his life. While he was living in caves and fleeing from one town to another, he heard that the Philistines were attacking an Israelite place called Keilah. Though it wasn't David's responsibility to go, and he had very few men with him, he inquired of God whether he should go and fight the Philistines. God answered by promising to "give the Philistines into your hand" (1 Sam. 23:5). David and his men saved the people of Keilah, took the Philistines' livestock, and killed many Philistines. They were successful because they consistently sought the Lord's will and obeyed his call.

506. David eventually went to live in the land of the Philistines in order to avoid Saul's attempts to kill him. During one occasion, while David and his men were intent on fighting Israel with the Philistines, the Amalekites came and raided David's own refuge, stealing all the women and children and plundering the place before burning it. David and his men were distraught, but they again sought God's leading. God assured David of the victory and so the warrior pursued the Amalekites. God gave the group into their hand, and the Israelites recovered everything—no single person or thing was missing from the Israelites' recovered belongings! (1 Sam. 30:19).

507. The Philistines were finally routed completely when King David sought God's leading and overtook them in battle with God leading the first assault against the Philistines. This was shortly after the Israelites overtook Jerusalem and the Jebusites and made that city David's city.

508. One of the most interesting motivations for a battle can be found in 2 Samuel 10:4. King David had sent a group of men to express Israel's sympathy over the death of the king of the Ammonites, a group that had lived in peace with Israel. The men were humiliated via this method: Half of each of their beards were shaved and their garments were cut around the buttocks (a sign saved for degrading prisoners of war). The shaving of the beards was considered an insult of the deepest kind. Beards were only shaved as signs of deep mourning. The Ammonites knew David would not accept such an action, and so they hired more soldiers to fight against Israel, but God delivered his people and made those other nations subject to Israel and at peace with God's people.

509. Battles naturally took many lives on both sides of the fighting. Such losses couldn't always be avoided, and the kings who waged wars knew it. David was one such king. He purposefully had Uriah, the husband of Bathsheba, put at the front of the battle in order that this innocent man might be killed and David's adultery with Bathsheba hidden. Uriah was a loyal soldier and went where he was directed. God knew what David had done and didn't let this offense go unpunished (the child born to David and Bathsheba died as a result). God consistently demonstrated his awareness of Israel's spiritual state.

510. "Twenty-four in all." One of those who fell against Israel was said to have twelve fingers and twelve toes. Four descendants of Rapha, all giants perhaps, also fell against Israel (2 Sam. 21:20–22). These were Philistines whom God delivered into Israel's hands.

511. Prayers to God for deliverance often preceded battles. David's psalms lament his pain and sorrow over enemies coming after him. Psalm 54 is one such plea: "Save me, O God, by your name; vindicate me by your might. Hear my prayer, O God; listen to the words of my mouth. Strangers are attacking me; ruthless men seek my life—men without regard for God. Surely God is my help; the LORD is the one who sustains me" (vv. 1–4).

13

Through Poetry, Song, and Lament

512. The books of poetry. Job, Psalms, Proverbs, Ecclesiastes, and Song of Solomon make up the Bible's books of poetry. Sometimes these are also called the "wisdom writings." All demonstrate Israel's need to commune with God through prayer and worship. Though they were supremely blessed, the Hebrews suffered through many difficulties and often called out to God for mercy. Their prayers were answered and they would then praise God for his faithfulness.

513. Hebrew poetry is picturesque and vivid. The rhythm or cadence to Hebrew poetry is lost to some degree in the translation, but it is filled with concrete images and deep emotion. These five books of poetry aren't just a change in style from previous books; the subject matter shifts as well. Wisdom takes center stage with these five books, therefore they are called the "wisdom literature" of the Bible.

514. Job is a book of both lament and praise. Whenever the troubling question of "Why do bad things happen to good people?" comes up, Job is the first to come to mind. Satan uses Job to try and prove a point to God that without God's protective covering over his people, they would fall away. Satan ultimately failed in his efforts. Though many ills happened to Job, he did not curse God or turn from the difficulties. As he states in Job 2:10, "Shall we accept good from God, and not trouble?"

515. Job is never identified as a Jew, and he wasn't a king, but his book fits with the poetic books of both King David and King Solomon. Job is thought to have lived in the Arabian Desert somewhere between Babylon and the Holy Land during the years of exile. So the Book of Job might fit more easily near Exodus!

516. God valued Job's faithfulness greatly, and though the heavenly Father did give Satan permission to harm what belonged to Job and eventually to harm his very person, he did not give Satan everything. Job's eternal life was already signed and sealed—God said, "There is no one on earth like [Job]; he is blameless and upright, a man who fears God and shuns evil" (Job 1:8). It can be difficult to resolve why God would put one of his children into such a predicament, and, like us, Job had the same questions.

517. Why did God allow Satan such opportunity? Satan accused God of being foolish; the great deceiver claimed that Job was only righteous and "faithful" because it helped him receive great blessing. In essence, Satan undermined the godliness of a redeemed man. If Satan could prove that Job's godliness was truthfully a self-serving sin, then redemption would be an impossibility. Satan wanted to show that this was indeed the case, and that ultimately, God's system is flawed. God allowed Satan to trouble Job because it was necessary in order to silence Satan. However, God is in control—he puts limits on how far Satan may go.

518. Job remained faithful to God. Job's friends told him that his sin was causing the problems, that God would not allow such suffering if he had been faithful. His wife told him to curse God and die. Job was left alone with his thoughts but would not turn his back on God. He cried out because he felt alienated from God, chided God for being unjust, and cursed the day of his birth, but he would not curse God. What pained Job most was God's apparent alienation from him—a sign that it is not earthly pain or misery we should fear, but the spiritual pain of separation from our heavenly Father.

519. Job won an audience with God. It is truly magnificent what God has to say to his child in chapters 38–42. God's sovereignty is firmly established, as is his faithfulness. Job's friends are chastised for their lack of faith, Job and God's relationship is completely restored, and Job is blessed even more in the second part of his life than he had been in the first.

520. Psalms. While Jews and Christians share the entire Hebrew Scriptures, or Old Testament, Psalms is the most emotionally and intensely shared book of Hebrew Scripture. Jews know many of the Psalms and individual verses by heart. Jesus often quoted or referred to the Psalms. Martin Luther called the Book of Psalms "a Bible in miniature." The 150 "rosaries" later instituted by the Roman Catholic Church are in honor of the 150 Psalms.

521. The Psalms chronicle both the joys and sorrows of God's people. They are timeless and demonstrate even today what it is to be a child of God: "Sing to the Lord, you saints of his; praise his holy name. For his anger lasts only a moment, but his favor lasts a lifetime; weeping may remain for a night, but rejoicing comes in the morning" (Ps. 30:4–5).

522. David was more than a great warrior. He was a musician who played the eight-stringed harplike instrument known as the lyre. He was also a great poet who composed about half of the Psalms. David used many descriptions of animals, birds, and plant life in the Psalms to portray poetic images. His songs were full of lament as well as praise. They were his prayers to the Lord.

523. "Oh, that I had the wings of a dove! I would fly away and be at rest." David, weighed down by his duties, must have wished he could take flight from his tasks. He might have selected almost any bird to express this wish in Psalm 55, yet he chose the dove for a particular reason. The former shepherd knew that while most birds can fly, only doves can take off with a sudden burst of speed and sustain their powerful flight for a long distance.

524. The shortest psalm (117) has just two verses, and the longest psalm is just two chapters later (119). It is also the longest chapter in the Bible, and longer than some whole Bible books—such as Obadiah, Philemon, and Jude.

525. The Book of Psalms is really five different books of songs and poems, all connecting our relationship to God.

Book 1	Psalms 1–41
Book 2	Psalms 42–72
Book 3	Psalms 73–89
Book 4	Psalms 90–106
Book 5	Psalms 107–150

526. It appears that this collection was begun as something of a hymnbook for temple worship in Jerusalem. Words such as *selah, maskil,* and *miktam* are found throughout the book to give direction to those who would speak or chant these psalms in public worship.

527. The Penitential Psalms is the title given to seven psalms that express deep repentance over sin: Psalms 7, 32, 38, 51, 102, 130, and 143. All but two are attributed to King David—most notably Psalm 51, which is his lament over committing adultery with Bathsheba.

528. The Messianic Psalms are Old Testament psalms that relate information about the coming Messiah, and were generally quoted by the Lord Jesus or the New Testament writers in reference to him. These include Psalms 22, 40, 41, 45, 69, 72, and 118.

529. The Psalms of Ascent were sung by Jewish pilgrims as they traveled upward from the surrounding areas of Palestine to the city of Jerusalem for festivals. The songs tell of looking up to the hills, seeing the walls of Jerusalem, and observing the many people gathering together to worship, and they end with a joyous shout of praise as the pilgrims finally arrive at the gates of the temple.

530. Acrostic poems are found throughout Jewish literature. Psalm 119, the longest chapter in the Bible, is an acrostic poem—every new stanza begins with the successive letter of the Hebrew alphabet. Psalm 112 is similar, each line beginning with the next letter of the alphabet. This was not only poetic, but aided in the memorization of the psalm.

531. Knowing it all. Solomon spoke over three thousand proverbs and wrote more than a thousand songs, some of which come down to us in the Books of Proverbs and the Song of Solomon. This son of David found favor with God and was given great wisdom, yet he too fell away from God. Different stages of his personal walk can be seen throughout his writings.

532. Proverbs. Some proverbs are strung together in a meaningful sequence, while others are independent of each other and need to be "unpacked" by the reader. The opening chapters of Proverbs contain extended proverbs progressing with each verse. Shorter bits of wisdom form chapters 10 and following. Proverbs leaves no ambiguity over the contrast between the righteous and the wicked.

533. The call of wisdom is made throughout the first ten chapters of Proverbs. Solomon, who was given great wisdom from God, says in Proverbs 8:22 that wisdom was the first creation of God. Solomon always refers to wisdom in the feminine sense: "She calls out . . ."

534. Solomon was the wisest man who ever lived; he was "wiser than all men" (1 Kings 4:31). God had asked him what he wanted more than anything, and Solomon asked for wisdom in order to better rule the people of Israel. His wisdom was unsurpassed, and the people lived very well under his rule. A beautiful temple was even built, but sadly, many of the Israelites, including Solomon, eventually began sacrificing to other gods. God raised up armies to fight against him and his people, but he made a decision not to take the nation from Solomon's rule. He would spare Solomon for his father, David's, sake. Instead Israel would be lost during the reign of Solomon's son, Rehoboam.

535. Ecclesiastes. If Job reads like a play, and Psalms like poetry, and Proverbs like a book of maxims, then Ecclesiastes reads like an essay or the musings of an old man. Its subject is the vanity of life. The book approaches Job's question from the opposite side: If this universe is governed by a moral God, why doesn't everything make sense?

536. It is believed that Solomon wrote Ecclesiastes. Solomon's struggle through this book to understand the purpose behind everything comes to a very strong conclusion. Essentially, God has ordered life for his own purpose, not man's. As a result, the worry and desire that cause people to constantly seek more in life—money, peace, happiness—are best served by turning to God. God controls everything, and man should know his limitations.

537. "**To the man who pleases him,** God gives wisdom, knowledge and happiness, but to the sinner he gives the task of gathering and storing up wealth to hand it over to the one who pleases God" (Eccles. 2:26). Striving after things is not where meaning is to be found, concludes Solomon. He calls it "a chasing after the wind."

538. Ecclesiastes's conclusion? "Fear God and keep his commandments, for this is the whole duty of man" (Eccles. 12:13). We should enjoy what God has given us, live in the Word, work hard and well, strive for righteousness, and enjoy God and the relationship we have with him!

539. Song of Solomon. Plain and simple, this book is an erotic love poem. The writing resembles Egyptian love poetry and Arabic wedding songs that praise the charm and beauty of the bride. The traditional interpretation, in both Judaism and Christianity, is that these love poems represent Yahweh's love for Israel as well as establishing God's high regard for male-female love and sexuality.

540. Some of the images are so mature that Jewish boys were not allowed to read Song of Solomon until they attained adulthood. Many people have questioned its place in Scripture, but Jewish leaders decided in ancient times that the book is allegorical—the man chasing a woman is a depiction of God pursuing sinful Israel. In medieval times, Christian scholars suggested that the book also represented Christ pursuing the church.

541. "Song of Songs" means "the greatest of songs" and is about the "God of gods and Lord of lords." It is believed Solomon wrote this book; however, others maintain that there were multiple authors for this unique book of Scripture.

542. Though it is a relatively short book, Song of Songs is a full and complete book. The voice of the beloved character (the one who is loved, such as Israel) is the one most heard from throughout. Through five meetings with the beloved, the lover is asked for first a kiss and ultimately for complete intimacy.

14

His Mouthpieces

543. The books of prophecy. This section of the Bible is composed of seventeen books beginning with Isaiah and ending with Malachi, closing out the Old Testament. Like the books of poetry, these books don't extend the time line of Israel's history; rather, they fill in the one laid down by the books of history. Apart from Job, most of the books of poetry were associated with the kings of Israel's glory days. By contrast, the books of prophecy were associated mainly with the period of Israel's decline and fall.

544. Prophets and priests played an important role in early Israel, though many of the prophets do not have books named after them. These godly men served as messengers from God to the people. The prophets and priests received orders from God and acted on them.

545. Prophecy in the Old Testament was not so much a telling of the future as it was an urgent statement made on behalf of God to his people. Certain elements of Hebrew prophecy spoke of the future in terms that human behavior could not change, but most of it offered God's people a choice and often stated the harsh consequences if the Israelites chose to disobey. Biblical prophecy emphasizes the kind of living that secures a happy future and warns against behavior that clouds the future.

546. Both the Major Prophets (Isaiah, Jeremiah, Ezekiel, and Daniel) and the Minor Prophets ("the twelve") are organized in historical order. However, this doesn't mean the minor prophets follow the major ones in history; they coexisted. Hosea, for example, was a contemporary of Isaiah. Since the fall of Jerusalem is dated by historians at 586 B.C., all the books of prophecy—major and minor—can be dated within a century or two of that date.

547. Moses said God would raise up prophets like him in the generations to follow. And God did. Generally keeping a low profile, the prophets did not possess administrative power like the kings. They didn't have a place in the tabernacle or temple rituals like the priests. They simply spoke the mind of God as it was given to them. Unlike the kingship and the priesthood, the position of prophet could not be passed on to one's descendants. God individually chose each one.

548. Elijah trusted God completely, so much so that when King Ahab, a later king, appointed prophets to worship the false god Baal, Elijah told him no more rain would fall. Three years after the drought began, when Israel was literally starving, Elijah had a contest with the Baal prophets to see which entity would answer their prayers—God or the false god Baal. The people were brought to their senses by the sign of a soaked altar bursting into flames, and they came back to God.

549. As one of only two men who never died, Elijah was truly a special prophet of God. Enoch, a man who walked with God, was the other man who didn't die. Elijah was taken up to heaven in a chariot of fire, but before he was taken he appointed Elisha, his servant, to succeed him.

550. Not a popular group. Israel's prophets were not the type of people to include on your party invitation list. The Hebrew prophets denounced evil, corruption, and immorality. They brought "bad" news, and people steered clear of them for the most part.

551. At the forefront. In the period of the divided kingdom, the focus of the Bible books moved away from the kings to the exploits of a series of "prophets," those who spoke on the behalf of God after receiving divine messages through dreams or visions. Prophets tried to counsel—usually with little success—the rulers and people of Israel and Judah. The prophets became crucial biblical characters who overshadowed the kings and took their message to the entire nation.

552. In Jewish history, law, and theology, Ezra is a character of great significance. Some Hebrew scholars rank him second only to Moses as a law giver and prophet, and he's considered by many as the second founder (after Moses) of the Jewish nation. Not only did Ezra reinstate the Law and temple worship practices, he required that all Jewish men get rid of their foreign wives and children. Ezra ends poignantly with the words, "All these had married foreign women, and some of them had children by these wives" (10:44).

553. Hosea is considered the first in the line of minor prophets. This is largely because his and the other minor prophets' books are short in length compared to Isaiah, Jeremiah, or Ezekiel. According to the recorded dates in Hosea, his ministry began shortly after that of Amos, and both of them were active before the fall of Jerusalem in 586 B.C.

554. Gomer, Hosea's adulterous wife, is a symbol of God's wayward people. God told Hosea to marry this wayward wife in order to further drive home the point of his message to Israel given through Hosea. Israel was rebellious and wicked, and worshiped other gods. God's nation was not to do these things under any circumstances, and though he was angered, God continued to love his people. Hosea was told to behave in a similar manner with Gomer. Each time she strayed, God's prophet was to bring her back home.

555. The message of Hosea to the Israelites used even the names of the three children Gomer bore. Hosea gave them names representative of how God felt about Israel. The children are a symbol of the results of the sin reaped by Israel for falling away from God—Gomer was unfaithful and the children were the fruit of her adultery. God told Hosea to name the children accordingly: Jezreel, meaning "God scatters"; Lo-Ruhamah, meaning "not loved"; and Lo-Ammi, meaning something similar to "not my people, and I am not your God."

556. God wants his people to repent. God wants to claim Israel for his own. He wants to call these children "his," "loved," and "my people." Through all of Gomer's waywardness, Hosea is not told to seek a divorce. Always he is instructed to reconcile with her, to bring her home, to love her. Hosea's life example is a symbol of what God continually did for his people. It would take exile for Israel to finally listen and repent, but God never forgot about them or stopped loving them.

557. The prophet Amos was the first prophet to have his words written down. His ministry occurred sometime during the years of 793–740 B.C. It is thought that most of his main prophesying occurred between 760 and 750 B.C. Where Hosea spoke of God's mercy, love, and forgiveness for his people, Amos spoke of God's justice and righteousness.

558. Israel worshiped God in a pagan manner—sacred altars and even the temple were given touches of the pagans. God's people went through the motions and did the rituals God required of them and then lived exactly as they wanted to. The result was an immoral society far from what God's people were called to be. As a result, Amos preached about true piety and social justice.

559. Micah lived after Amos and Hosea. He prophesied of a future king who would be born in Bethlehem. He looked forward to that time as the current kings he suffered with consistently led the people toward idol worship and other forms of sin.

560. Nahum's name means "comfort." His book was written for Judah and served to comfort them with a prophecy of Nineveh's future destruction. Nineveh was the capital city of Assyria, which had already taken possession of the Northern kingdom of Israel.

Judah feared they were next. The Assyrians were a brutal people known for their ferocious wars.

561. Nahum's book demonstrates that God is sovereign over all nations, not just his own. The destinies of Assyria, Babylon, Rome, and Israel and Judah were all under God's control. That God had Judah carried off by Babylon and Israel carried off by Assyria was all part of his plan for his people.

562. The longest prophetic book in Hebrew Scripture, Isaiah has played a central role for Christians and has even been called "the fifth Gospel" because so many of the book's prophecies were fulfilled in the life of Jesus. This book has also had an impact on our language.

563. Many well-worn phrases were born in the Book of Isaiah. Besides providing Handel with wonderful lyrics, Isaiah has yielded phrases commonly used even today:

"White as snow"
"Neither shall they learn war anymore"
"The people that walked in darkness"
"And a little child shall lead them"
"They shall mount up with wings as eagles"
"Be of good courage"
"Like a lamb to the slaughter"

564. The Servant Songs are the passages of Scripture describing an innocent man who endures great pain (Isaiah 42, 49, 50, 52, and 53). Many Jewish scholars did not know what to do with these passages and could not reconcile them to the images of the Messiah coming as a mighty king. But Christians from earliest times have applied them to Jesus Christ, who suffered greatly for the sins of all mankind.

565. Jeremiah is the longest book in the Bible, containing more words than any other Bible book. This prophet was unpopular largely because his messages of Judah's coming destruction were different from what the false prophets were telling the people—that all was well, God was pleased with them, and peace would reign.

Through Jeremiah God demonstrated that judgment would come for disobedience, but that even judgment has boundaries. Israel would be subject to Babylon, but only for a time—seventy years. God would not abandon them.

566. Also known as the "weeping prophet," Jeremiah's outpourings to God reveal that even prophets had difficulties with their relationship with God. In chapter 4 of the book that bears his name, he cries out to God: "Oh, my anguish, my anguish! I writhe in pain. Oh, the agony of my heart!" (v. 19). Jeremiah was honest with God when he was frustrated—on several occasions he questioned God's plan for himself, God's plan for his people, and ultimately God's faithfulness. Yet God used him and made him a great prophet.

567. Habakkuk is thought to have been a prophet around the time of Jeremiah. He struggled with how God would want his people, despite how badly they were behaving, to come under the influence of an even more ungodly people—the Babylonians. God was faithful to his prophet and assured Habakkuk to trust him for the answer.

568. The Book of Lamentations may have been written by the prophet Jeremiah, but this fact is not certain. Interestingly the Hebrew title for the book is *eykah*, which means "How . . . !" Simply put, Lamentations describes the horrendous loss of Jerusalem, the temple, and the exile of Judah's inhabitants to Babylon. As Jerusalem was destroyed in 586 B.C., this book was likely written shortly after.

569. Lamentations is a grievous statement of all the ills that befell this people as a result of their turning away from God. It is the only book of the Bible that consists *solely* of laments. Though the book begins with lament, it ends with heartfelt repentance, as it should. The author is very clear that though Babylon is the enemy carrying out the destruction, God has truly destroyed his people's city and allowed them to be carried off.

570. The final verses of Lamentations demonstrate exactly how Israel responded to God's judgment: "Restore us to yourself, O LORD, that we may return; renew our days as of old unless you have utterly rejected us and are angry with us beyond measure" (Lam. 5:21–22).

571. Ezekiel was living in exile in Babylon when Jerusalem fell. His prophetic work was to a people that had been exiled with him since 596 B.C. Ezekiel was served some truly bitter news that directly affected his work as well. God told his prophet that Ezekiel's wife was going to die, and soon. The prophet was instructed not to mourn openly for his wife, just as Israel was not to grieve openly for the temple that they had lost as a nation.

572. God's prophets were tested with difficulty like all of Israel was during this period of loss. They were God's voices and stayed with the people to tell them what their Lord had to say, even in the midst of grief, exile, and personal pain. They also passed judgments from the Lord on to others. Ezekiel pronounced God's judgment on seven different nations while he was in Babylon.

573. Ezekiel's message is filled with the theme of Israel as "the holy people"; a people set apart. With Israel's departure from worshiping God, the nation became unclean and defiled the temple, city, and land. God responded by withdrawing from his people and allowing national destruction of all that he had given them. God had no choice but to destroy that which had become unclean.

574. Daniel is considered a book more of a statesman than a prophet. As a result, Jewish scholars do not place this book among the prophetic books. However, since Daniel had the gift of prediction, the New Testament calls him a "prophet" (Matt. 24:15). Daniel saw many symbols in his prophetic visions, and he often recorded them without attempting to interpret what they meant.

575. Daniel contains a fair amount of apocalyptic material. Whether it is to be interpreted literally or symbolically, it served as an encouragement to Israel. God's prophets were the closest thing the people had to a direct line to God. Through Daniel God told the people that there would be an end to their exile; there would be good times again. Daniel's prophetic themes are largely about God's sovereignty and appear in Revelation: "The kingdom of the world has become the kingdom of our Lord and of his Christ, and he will reign for ever and ever" (Rev. 11:15; see Dan. 2:44; 7:27).

15

Pointing to Christ

576. Jesus can be seen in the Old Testament through many characters in the Bible who are pictures of Christ. Long before Jesus' birth in Bethlehem, God's plan for his son was in place. The Old Testament patriarchs, prophets, and heroic figures are all linked to Christ and point to the Messiah.

577. Another word used to describe these "pictures" is the word *type*. Though this word isn't in the Bible, it comes from the study of types, or typology. *Type* comes from the Greek word *typos*, which is translated as "figure" or "shadow." These original types are historically accurate, but they also foreshadow another person, incident, or event to happen in the future.

578. "Although the Bible contains no visual picture or portrait in the generally accepted sense of the word, it is filled with word pictures, and all these have as their central figure a Person, and that Person is the Lord Jesus Christ, the Son of God and Son of Man, the Savior of Sinners."—Dr. M. R. DeHaan

579. "And beginning with Moses and all the Prophets, [Jesus] explained to them [the disciples] what was said in all the Scriptures concerning himself" (Luke 24:27).

580. Adam is the first picture of Christ that Genesis reveals. Paul speaks of this portrait of Christ in Ephesians 5. When Adam was in a deep sleep, God took one of his ribs and created Eve. The apostle Paul speaks of Christians being members of Jesus' body and his bones. Paul quotes how a man shall leave his family and be joined to his wife. Paul says "this is a profound mystery—but I am talking about Christ and the church" (Eph. 5:32). The apostle is alluding to the fact that Jesus left God's house to be joined to his bride, the church, and that he too was put to sleep, only his three-day sleep would result in resurrection. As Adam suffered a wound to his side, Christ's side too was wounded, but his blood is our redemption.

581. Abel, the son of Adam and Eve, is also a picture of Jesus Christ. Abel was obedient and followed God's instructions regarding sacrifice. His gift of the best lambs in his flock was the exact opposite of Cain's sacrifice—essentially a poor gift of his own hands as a gardener, a picture of selfishness and an attempt to gain favor through a personal work rather than a wholehearted sacrifice. Abel foreshadowed the coming Messiah, who would do everything according to God's commandments yet still be rejected and ultimately killed by his own people because of his personal faithfulness to God. As Cain slew Abel, so the Jews would demand Jesus' death.

582. Another demonstration of Abel's foreshadowing has to do with his profession. Abel was a shepherd, the very first the world had ever seen. Jesus called himself the good shepherd who "lays down his life for the sheep" (John 10:11).

583. The story of Noah and the ark yields some interesting analysis as a type of Christ. The ark itself is a type of Christ! God gave Noah every detail of how it was to be built, from its dimensions to its purpose in protecting Noah and his family from the judgment that awaited the rest of the world. Likewise God planned every minute detail of how Jesus would redeem God's people; not a single detail was left to man. As the big boat brought earthly salvation for Noah, so Christ brings eternal salvation for all who believe in him. As the ark had but one door, so Christ is the door to God—he is the only way we may gain forgiveness for our sins and come to the Father.

584. We have a responsibility just as Noah did. As Noah was safe in the ark, God had given him duties and responsibilities. Noah was to care for the animals and keep things orderly. God had protected him within the ark, just as we are protected (redeemed) within Christ. God has responsibilities for us too; we are to care for one another.

585. Isaac, the son of the patriarch Abraham, is perhaps one of the most vivid foreshadows of Jesus Christ. Just as Jesus was miraculously conceived by the Holy Spirit through Mary, Isaac was a miracle given to Abraham and Sarah in their old age. Both were the "child of promise." Abraham had been told his offspring would be great in number, yet Sarah was barren into her nineties. As Isaac was a miracle, he also points to the miraculous virgin birth of our Savior.

586. The call for Abraham to sacrifice Isaac is another foreshadowing of Christ's earthly existence. God commanded Abraham to sacrifice his only son as a sign of obedience to God's commands, as all sacrifices were. Christ was the supreme atoning sacrifice, putting an end to the need to make sacrifices to God. As Isaac carried the wood for the altar he was to be sacrificed on, Christ carried the cross he was to be crucified on. Yet Isaac did not serve as a sacrifice as Jesus did, because only Christ can redeem us. God provided a ram for the sacrifice in Isaac's stead, causing Isaac to be saved from death.

587. Jacob is the next patriarch and type of Christ. The famous story of the "stealing of the birthright" is a foreshadowing of the first and second Adams' experience. As Adam was given dominion first, before any other, so also was Esau given dominion by his birthright. Yet just as Adam forfeited his right, so also did Esau. Those rights passed on to the second Adam, Christ, and to Esau's brother, Jacob, who was to carry on the covenant with God as a patriarch of Israel.

588. Joseph, Jacob's favorite son, is another figure whose foreshadowing is very vivid. Joseph was well-known for his ability to foretell the future. Though his brothers found his dreams offensive, Joseph did have the ability to correctly interpret dreams. Jesus told of his own future too, and he consistently angered those who heard him do it. The Pharisees were constantly angry at what they considered blasphemy. Joseph's brothers and those who were offended by Jesus' prophecies are the same image.

589. Just as Joseph came to his own people (his brothers) and was rejected, so Jesus was rejected by his own people. Just as the brothers of Joseph were jealous of his beautiful coat and stripped it off of him before they sold him to the peddlers heading to Egypt, Jesus was stripped of the robe he wore before he was crucified. Soldiers cast lots for it because it was a specially woven item and too expensive to be cut into parts.

590. Joseph is also the deliverer; he is an early picture of what Christ will be for all people. Joseph delivered his brothers from starvation. As a high-ranking official of Egypt, he saved them. Christ also saved us, but just as Joseph's brothers had to go about it in a specific manner, humbly, seeking favor, so also we must be humble and approach what Christ has done for us in a specific manner. We do not save ourselves, because only Christ can save us. Joseph saved his brothers from starvation, because he was the only one who could.

591. Moses was also a deliverer. God called him to lead the Israelites out of Egypt in a mass exodus. Pointing to Jesus, Moses is a great man, but he is not the supreme deliverer. From our fallen state, Jesus redeems us and makes us forgiven, bringing us into a new and ultimately heavenly relationship with the Father. Moses brought enslaved Israel out of a foreign land. As God called Moses, God called Jesus.

592. "When Israel was a child, I loved him, and out of Egypt I called my son" (Hosea 11:1). "So he [Joseph, Jesus' earthly father] got up, took the child and his mother during the night and left for Egypt, where he stayed until the death of Herod. And so was fulfilled what the Lord had said through the prophet: 'Out of Egypt I called my son'" (Matt. 2:14–15). Matthew was under the divine inspiration of the Holy Spirit and saw the history of Israel being replayed in the life of Jesus. As Israel went to Egypt in its infancy, so Jesus went to Egypt in his own infancy.

593. David was the Lord's anointed and suffered because of it. He and his greater Son, Jesus, demonstrate how David is a type of Christ figure (Matt. 1:1; Rev. 22:16). Jesus' ministry was plagued by difficulties, as was David's role both before and after he became king. The common theme is of the servant of the Lord enduring scorn and suffering trials in the name of the Lord.

594. Psalm 69 demonstrates this point as David cries out to God: "For I endure scorn for your sake, and shame covers my face. I am a stranger to my brothers, an alien to my own mother's sons; for zeal for your house consumes me, and the insults of those who insult you fall on me" (Ps. 69:7–9). The Gospel of John makes reference to these verses.

595. "The Bible is a collection of portraits of one supreme Person who overshadows all the rest of the pictures. The central object of this Bible Album is Jesus Christ. . . . He is the central figure on every page, and the other pictures grouped about Him are added only to bring into bolder relief the loveliness, the superlative beauty, the infinite perfection of the Man of the Book, the Lord Jesus."—Dr. M. R. DeHaan

16

New Times

596. "To him give all the prophets witness." Truly, God had been telling his people about the coming Savior long before Jesus was ever born. Micah foretells Jesus' birth, Zechariah tells of how he will eventually reign as King over all the earth. Joel describes the day of judgment and what part Jesus will play in it.

597. The four Gospels follow closely in the tradition of the books of history we saw in the Old Testament—words are spoken and deeds are done. Little is told of the inward thoughts and motivations of the various people in the stories. The Gospels tell how Jesus was born as a descendant of David, an essential requirement of the Messiah according to the prophecies of Scripture.

598. The Gospel of Matthew was written by a former tax collector named Matthew. His book covers the lineage of Jesus and also tells the story of much of his ministry, including the Beatitudes.

599. Mark details Jesus' service to those he called and preached to. Jesus' portrayal as the great servant can be found in this Gospel, written by someone about whom we know very little.

600. Luke opens his Gospel by saying that "many" had attempted to write an account of Jesus' life and ministry, but that he himself is doing so because God has given him "perfect understanding of all things from the very first" (Luke 1:3 KJV). God not only gave the Gospel writers firsthand exposure as eyewitnesses to the events of Jesus' ministry, but also perfect understanding. Luke is especially forthright about Christ the man.

601. John, perhaps the most famous book of the whole Bible in terms of its saving message, is a description of both Christ's deity and his redeeming work for sinners. The Gospel was written by the "disciple whom Jesus loved," John.

602. The four Gospels therefore tell of all aspects of Jesus: Matthew of his right to be called "King," Mark of his title as "Greatest Servant," Luke of his completely human nature, and John of his being the Savior of the World—God's only Son.

603. Jesus Christ, more than any other figure or historical happening mentioned, is the most important figure in the Bible. The Old Testament prophesies about his coming and his death, and the New Testament sees him born, establish a ministry, and eventually sacrifice himself for all who believe in him.

604. Many incidents in the Old Testament point to Christ: Abel's lamb was a type of Christ. So was Abraham's willing offering of his son, Isaac, for sacrifice. The Passover lamb in Egypt was a type of Christ. Even the scarlet cord the prostitute Rahab hung in her window is a symbol of Christ!

605. Jesus met all manner of people—and accepted them all if they repented of their sins. Harlots, tax collectors, liars, cheats, the infirm, the diseased all received kind words, healing, and a message of hope.

606. Obedience to laws without a sense of mercy is empty of spiritual value. Several times Jesus quoted the prophets who had said, "God desires mercy more than sacrifice." He reserved a special anger for those he called the "scribes and Pharisees," a group that might be loosely called "lawyers." Matthew's term for Pharisees is "hypocrites," a term in Greek that applied to actors or people who were pretenders, people who said one thing but did another.

607. The Beatitudes is the well-known portion of Scripture from Christ's Sermon on the Mount in which he blesses certain types of people. Matthew 5 records that Jesus blessed the poor in spirit, those who mourn, the meek, those who hunger and thirst for righteousness, the merciful, the pure in heart, the peacemakers, and those who are persecuted for righteousness' sake—all of which describe the people who would populate the kingdom of God. However, the actual word *beatitude* doesn't appear in Scripture. It's from the Latin word for "blessed," and was made popular by the Vulgate.

608. Parables are stories Jesus used to convey spiritual truth. They were essentially comparisons: "The kingdom of heaven is like a treasure hidden in a field" or "Everyone who hears these words and puts them into practice is like a wise man who built a house." While Jesus' concrete images made the parables memorable, they also puzzled people who could not always follow Christ's meaning.

609. Biblical miracles are found in both the Old and New Testaments. Many show God's power over nature, while others are a sign of his mercy and love for those who fear him. These events are supernatural and can only be the work of God.

610. Miracles demonstrate God's hand intervening in earthly affairs in extraordinary ways. But New Testament miracles tend to be "personal" miracles, as opposed to miracles affecting the entire nation, such as the plagues on Egypt or the crossing of the Red Sea. Apart from his own miraculous birth, resurrection, and transfiguration, Jesus performed more than thirty-five miracles in the Gospels.

611. The parable of the sower, found in Matthew 13, likens sharing the gospel to a farmer scattering seed. Seed sown on the path is eaten by birds—which the Lord explains is similar to what occurs when a hearer doesn't understand the message. Satan snatches it away so that it cannot have an impact on the hearer's life. Seed scattered on rocky soil sprouts but dies because it cannot set its roots—this is likened to someone who initially believes the gospel but falls away from the faith due to persecution. Some seed grows but is choked out by thorns—a depiction of the person whose belief is undermined by worldly concerns. But the good seed that grows is like the individual who hears the gospel, understands it, and chooses to follow Christ.

612. Water into wine. The first recorded miracle of Jesus occurs in John 2, when Christ was attending a wedding in the city of Cana and the hosts ran out of wine. Jesus had the servants fill six large jars with water, which miraculously turned into fine wine. As John records, "He thus revealed his glory, and his disciples put their faith in him" (2:11).

613. The parable of the mustard seed likens the kingdom of heaven to the smallest seed known in that part of the world. Though the seed is tiny, the plant grows to a great height. In the same way, though the church started small, it would grow rapidly and become a worldwide force throughout the rest of history.

614. The centurion's servant. Since Roman conquerors were hated by most Jewish citizens, it was generally forbidden for a Jew to enter a Roman's home. Thus when a God-fearing Roman centurion told Jesus that his servant was ill, he informed the Lord that Jesus didn't have to enter his home to perform the healing. Instead Christ could do it from a distance. Marveling at the man's faith, Jesus replied, "I have not found anyone in Israel with such great faith." Before the centurion could get home, his servant was healed.

615. The parable of the sheep and the goats is a picture of what will happen when Christ returns. Sheep symbolize believers; goats symbolize unbelievers. The sheep will be parted from the goats with a final destination of heaven. The goats will be sent to hell, the place of eternal punishment.

616. The transfiguration. A few days before his death, Jesus took Peter, James, and John up to a high mountain. There he was "transfigured" before them, his face "shone like the sun, and his clothes became as white as the light." Moses and Elijah, two of the handful of miracle workers in Scripture, then appeared with Jesus, and the voice of God announced, "This is my Son, whom I love; with him I am well pleased" (Matt. 17:5).

617. The parable of the lost sheep, in Matthew 18, is one of the sweetest stories of Jesus. In it he tells of a loving shepherd caring for a hundred sheep. If one gets lost, he will leave the ninety-nine to go find the one that is missing. In the same way, God is concerned about each person. He doesn't want anyone to be lost.

618. Jesus was well-received by the people as long as he was performing miracles and teaching, but they did not look to him as the King of kings. Sadly they were looking for an earthly king instead of a heavenly one. As a result, their love for Jesus was short-lived.

619. Satan tempted Christ and tried to weaken the Savior's resolve, but Jesus stood firm in his mission. Christ's ministry would ultimately lead to his death, and though Satan's temptations would have saved him great pain, he was faithful to his heavenly Father.

620. Jesus called special helpers to his aid in order to preach and teach and minister to the people. There were twelve disciples in all—Simon Peter, Andrew, James, John, Philip, Bartholomew, Thomas, Matthew, James, Thaddaeus, Simon the Zealot, and Judas Iscariot.

621. The Last Supper was a preparation for Jesus himself as he readied himself for the end, which he knew was near. He even confronted Judas Iscariot at the table. The Lord celebrated a final supper with his disciples, his most trusted companions. This special dinner was given to Christians in order to remember the sacrifice Jesus made for his people.

622. The words "Take and eat, this is my body," and "This is my blood of the covenant, which is poured out for many for the forgiveness of sins" originated with the Last Supper. Communion recalls the Last Supper and serves as one of two main ordinances, or sacraments, in the Christian church to this day.

623. Many first-century Jews died, just like Jesus, on a cross. Some estimates for the number of Jews crucified during this time for a variety of crimes run as high as one hundred thousand. But these crucifixions were not at the hand of other Jews. Crucifixion was exclusive to the Romans, and it was an extreme penalty generally reserved for cases of runaway slaves or rebellion against Rome.

624. The Seven Last Utterances are the final words spoken by Christ while on the cross. The four Gospels reveal different phrases, but grouped together they include: (1) "Today you will be with me in paradise" (spoken to the thief next to him). (2) "My God, my God, why have you forsaken me?" (3) "Father, forgive them, for they know not what they do." (4) "I thirst." (5) "Woman, behold your son. Son, behold your mother" (spoken to Mary and the disciple John). (6) "It is finished." (7) "Into your hands I commit my spirit."

625. Jesus commissioned his followers to preach the gospel to all people. His call to them brought the disciples and other faithful followers to begin the church. And through a history of almost two thousand years, the church has experienced persecution, misery, and separation. Yet never has it died and never will it fall, despite what might happen, for Christ is the head of his church. And his kingdom cannot fail!

626. The resurrection. The greatest of all miracles in the Christian faith is the fact that Jesus rose from the dead, conquering death and sin. The evidence for the resurrection as a historical fact (the empty tomb, the Roman guard, the eyewitness reports of those who were there, the lack of any other explanation) is overwhelming.

627. The resurrection of Jesus is the central story of all Christianity. After dying on the cross and being wrapped in a burial shroud and interred in a sealed tomb, Jesus rose from the dead—conquering death and offering the hope of eternal life to all who believe in him.

628. Christ ascended into heaven, on a cloud, to be with the Father until the time of his second coming and to "sit at the right hand of God." He will come again at "the last days" as the Bible writers prophesied. His message remains today for all who will believe in him and trust him as their personal Savior.

629. The apostles' letters are sometimes called epistles. The word *epistle* conveys a formal or public element to these letters. These last twenty-two books of the Bible were personal letters often specifying the names of both the sender and the recipients. The fact that no point is made of the authors' identities implies how unimportant the issue is. The apostles were charged with the responsibility of spreading Jesus' message faithfully, and that in and of itself gave the writings authority in the eyes of Christ's followers.

17

God's Church

630. **Until the Book of Acts,** the Bible primarily belonged to the Jewish people. Of the many radical elements of Jesus' message, one of the most radical was that he meant for it to apply to Gentiles (non-Jews) as well as Jews. When Jesus told his apostles to go to the ends of the world, he really meant it. This brisk narrative begins in Jerusalem and ends in Rome, symbolizing how Jesus took the faith of ancient Israel and opened it up to the whole world.

631. **The lists of disciples** differ slightly from one book to another. The Gospel of Matthew lists Simon, Andrew (Simon's brother), James and John (the Sons of Zebedee), Philip, Bartholomew, Thomas, Matthew the tax collector, James the son of Alphaeus, Thaddaeus, Simon the Cananite, and Judas Iscariot. Luke refers to

Simon as "the zealot" (a brand of political protestors) and mentions "Judas son of James" instead of Thaddaeus. Many of these men were pillars of the early church.

632. Peter was called Simon before Jesus renamed him and was prominent in the early church. Peter had a long history with the Lord; he denied Christ before the cock crowed three times but went on in faith following Christ's death and resurrection to become exactly what his new name meant: "the rock."

633. James and John, both sons of Zebedee, were brothers. They both were active in the early church. Both had been especially close to Jesus, being present at the transfiguration. It is strongly believed that John went on to write the Gospel of John.

634. Acts introduces the New Testament's second most influential figure (Jesus was the first!), an educated, pious Jew and tent maker named Saul. Born in what is now Turkey, Saul went to Jerusalem to learn from the esteemed rabbi Gamaliel, grandson of the legendary rabbi Hillel, the most prominent Pharisaic rabbi of the first century. Given authority by the high priest to arrest followers of Christ in Damascus for blasphemy, Saul vigorously persecuted early Christians. His name was changed to Paul after he experienced a transforming vision and conversion.

635. Paul developed a strategy for his traveling ministry that he followed through all his journeys. He generally moved farther westward from Israel with each mission. When he entered a city for the first time, he would look for a synagogue or other place where he could find the Jews of the city. In the first century A.D., Jews were dispersed throughout the world. Rarely did a city not have Jews who met together regularly. Sometimes synagogues were receptive to his message; at other times hearers were extremely hostile.

636. When Paul was arrested in Jerusalem for his "heretical" views, he demanded a trial in Rome before the emperor, his right as a Roman citizen.

637. Many other missionaries preached the gospel in the early years of the church. Their mission was to spread the word of Christ to all parts of the known earth, as they had been commissioned to do by Jesus before he returned to heaven. Thanks to their efforts,

Christianity gained a foothold quickly in nearly every part of the known world.

638. Barnabas was one of the earliest converts to Christianity and a close friend of Paul's. A Greek-speaking Jew from Cyprus, his real name was Joseph, but because he was an excellent teacher, his friends called him Barnabas, which means "son of encouragement." He accompanied Paul on the first missionary journey through Asia Minor.

639. Timothy was one of Paul's main helpers. Paul mentored the younger man through two letters (1 and 2 Timothy) and called him "my true son in the faith." Timothy also traveled on his own.

640. Philip became a missionary and was the first to preach the gospel to those living in Samaria. He is especially remembered for how he helped an Ethiopian read a passage from Isaiah. An angel directed him to go to the Ethiopian. Upon his arrival, they read the passage together. The foreigner asked to be baptized and became the first Ethiopian Christian.

641. Silas traveled as a missionary with Paul and Peter. He sang hymns joyously to Christ while imprisoned with Paul during the earthquake in Philippi. The jailer became a Christian because he was so moved by their display of faith. Silas was to Paul a "faithful brother."

642. Phoebe is one of the few women missionary figures of the New Testament. History indicates that it was not uncommon for women to be in leadership roles in the early church, though it was certainly not typical in Jewish synagogues. Phoebe traveled to Rome, most likely to bring Paul's letter to the Christians in that city.

643. Apollos was a Jew from Alexandria. He was actually a missionary before he met Paul. John the Baptist had mentored him and helped Apollos become a powerful preacher. He found help for his questions about Jesus in Corinth when he spoke with Priscilla and Aquila.

644. Roman subjects incorporated emperor worship into the local religion throughout the empire. In the provinces, leading citizens became priests in the imperial cult to cement their ties with Rome. (Augustus, however, exempted the Jews from the imperial cult.) Emperor worship continued as the official pagan religion of the empire until Christianity was recognized under the Emperor Constantine (A.D. 306–337).

645. Paul stayed longer in some cities than others. Some larger cities, such as Ephesus, became teaching centers through which he could reach the surrounding regions. Paul's goal was to teach his followers well enough so they could teach others. Those who were able to accept this role were called elders, overseers, and pastors. The focus, however, was not on building an organization, but on preaching the Word.

646. The excellent highway system constructed throughout the Mediterranean world by the Romans was traveled frequently by Paul. Built so Roman armies could move swiftly and their traders could deliver goods efficiently, the Roman roads also contributed to the spread of the Christian message.

647. Corinth was the main city of the Roman province of Greece. It held a large community of Christians, thanks in large part to the missionary work of the apostle Paul. Corinth was an immoral and highly cosmopolitan city. Calling someone a "Corinthian" was for many people another way of saying "prostitute." The Christians faced moral dilemmas and difficulties and were counseled by Paul in 1 and 2 Corinthians regarding these issues.

648. When the New Testament writers speak of "Asia," they are not referring to the whole continent of Asia as we know it. Rather they are speaking of the province of the Roman Empire known as "Asia," a piece of land in the vicinity of modern-day Turkey. This province's capital was Ephesus. This city received one of Paul's epistles, which we know as Ephesians. John makes note of the seven churches of the province of Asia when he writes the Book of Revelation.

649. Since many Jews traveled to Jerusalem for annual feasts, and since many apostles were on the road with Christ's message, Paul sometimes found that the gospel message had reached a town before he did. This was the case with Rome, the center of the world in its day. There were many disciples in this metropolis long before Paul reached it.

650. The gospel of Christ spread primarily by word of mouth. Sometimes the apostles would move on to another city only to receive a request for more teaching from the city they had recently left. So they would write letters to be read aloud to groups of individuals who met for teaching and encouragement. They also wrote letters while confined in prison.

651. The Agrapha is a phrase meaning "things not written." It was used in the early church to refer to sayings of Jesus that his followers remembered, but which were not written down in any of the Gospels. For example, in Acts 20:35, Paul quotes the Lord Jesus as saying, "It is more blessed to give than to receive." Those words can't be found in any of the Gospels, so apparently that is one of the things the Lord's followers remembered him saying, and they would cite him as the source even though it was never written down as such.

652. How do you tell the world the Good News if you don't speak their language? The disciples were gathered in an upper room when all of a sudden "tongues of fire" touched the followers. And they began to speak in other languages. Some people who saw them thought they were drunk. This was the arrival of the Holy Spirit whom Jesus had promised. The disciples could now go and spread the Word everywhere.

653. The early church grew as a "communistic" society in which everyone shared, according to the reports in Acts. A utopian state of harmony is depicted in these first days of the Christian community, although they were not yet called "Christians." A young man named Matthias was elected to replace Judas as one of the Twelve, and the group prospered and made collective decisions and enjoyed common ownership of goods, making the early Christians in Jerusalem a practical model for the kibbutz.

654. Seven young men were appointed in Acts 6 to see to the needs of the church people in order to free up the time of the disciples and eventual apostles. Stephen, a gifted speaker, was one of these men. He was a skilled debater and angered many who could not argue well with him or win him over. Eventually these men became so angry that Stephen was arrested and tried before the Sanhedrin.

655. Stephen was the first martyr of the church. A young Pharisee named Saul was present. Eventually Saul would be converted and receive the name Paul. His conversion is a sign of the wondrous grace God has in store for those who believe in him. Stephen died with a vision of Jesus in sight. He was at peace and thus incensed his captors even more. Before he died, Stephen said, "Lord, do not hold this sin against them."

656. The early church was not a perfect organization. Christians were as sinful then as they can be now. One of the earliest instances of this appears in Acts 5. Ananias and his wife, Sapphira, lied about the amount of compensation they received after selling a field. Had they not pretended to sell it for less, it wouldn't have mattered, but since they did lie in order to keep back money for themselves, God took them both. As Peter told them, "You have lied to the Holy Spirit!"

657. Another famous Ananias was Ananias of Damascus. When Paul was converted, he became blinded. Ananias was told to go to the house where Paul was staying. He did so, though he knew that the man Saul was coming to arrest Christians. He went as he was called, however. He prayed, and the newly converted Paul received his sight back.

658. Dorcas, who was also called Tabitha, received a miracle during the early days of the church. She lived in Joppa. She fell ill and then died. Her distressed friends sent for Peter, the "rock" of the church. He prayed for her even as she was dead! She was given her life back and sat up. Many of her friends became believers as a result of this miracle.

659. Cornelius was a Roman soldier stationed at Caesarea. He was a Gentile who had joined a synagogue in order to seek God. He was a "God fearer." An angel appeared to Cornelius one day and told him to send for Peter. When Peter came, Cornelius and his entire family learned about Jesus. They were baptized immediately and praised God.

660. Eutychus was named well. His name means "lucky." While he was listening to Paul preach, he fell out of a third-story window (he fell asleep) and was lying still and believed to be dead when they reached him. Paul embraced him and he was healed. He had been blessed, not lucky, but his name seems appropriate!

661. Philemon had an interesting conversion experience. He was a wealthy Christian from Colossae and was converted by his slave, Onesimus. Onesimus had run away and eventually met the apostle Paul and became a believer. Paul sent him back to his master, Philemon, and urged Philemon to receive him as a "beloved brother." Philemon did so and was also saved!

662. Lydia is one of the few women mentioned in the early church. She was a seller of purple cloth and a Gentile, but she sought God by going to a Jewish prayer center. She then met Paul and his fellow missionaries. She became converted and eventually she and her family and even their workers were baptized. Paul and his friends stayed in her house.

663. Stephanas and his entire household were the first Christians to convert during Paul's ministry in Achaia. As the church grew in that area, Stephanas took a more active role in caring for other new Christians. Paul was fond of him and his family and he especially enjoyed when Stephanas visited him in Ephesus.

664. Aquila and Priscilla were a tent-making couple from Corinth. They became Christians after listening to Paul preach. Dear friends of Paul, they supported him to the very end, even risking their lives for him. They were loved and known in many churches in Greece and Asia Minor.

665. Acts closes with Paul incarcerated and under house arrest in the imperial capital. He continued preaching the gospel and writing letters to the churches he had established. Acts says nothing more about Paul's appeal or ultimate fate, or that of Peter. Both eventually disappeared from the biblical account without any specific word of what happened to them. According to well-established tradition, both apostles were martyred during Emperor Nero's persecution of Christians after the great fire in Rome in A.D. 64.

666. Early Christians used the "holy kiss" as a sign of their concern and love for one another. Paul ends several of his epistles with reminders to "Greet one another with a holy kiss" (Rom. 16: 16). The holy kiss was most likely a peck on the cheek, much as might be used today to greet visiting family or friends.

18

The End—Revelation

667. Revelation. The longest of all the New Testament letters, "The Revelation to John" was addressed to seven specific communities, all located in Asia. There is overwhelming evidence that this book was written by the apostle John, the son of Zebedee. Like Hebrews, this book is built upon quotations and allusions to Old Testament passages (hundreds of references).

668. Patmos is where John wrote this final book. This small island is located off the coast of Turkey and is thought to have held a Roman penal colony. John was exiled there for his activities as a missionary of Christ.

669. Revelation was written just as Christians were entering an intense period of persecution. The second half of Nero's reign (A.D. 54–68) and the late years of Domitian's reign (A.D. 81–96) are mentioned several times. Most scholars date Revelation around A.D. 95.

670. John wrote mainly in response to the continuing growth of emperor worship being enforced by the Romans. Christians were naturally being pressured to proclaim Caesar as Lord, but John wrote to encourage them to resist such demands since they were signed and sealed in Christ and would be vindicated when Christ returned, an event John expected was imminent. He could not visit the churches in Asia Minor, as he had been exiled to the island of Patmos, so he wrote them a letter instead.

671. Revelation's theme. Perhaps a story of goodness and evil waging a cataclysmic battle in which goodness wins the decisive victory, Revelation is more often seen as a prophecy of end times. The use of bizarre, conflicting images was a practiced style in ancient times. It was called "apocalyptic," so the book is sometimes called the Apocalypse instead of Revelation. The meaning is actually the same, only "apocalypse" comes from a Greek root while "revelation" comes from a Latin root word.

672. There are four interpretations of Revelation. *Preterists* believe Revelation's events have already taken place; they understand Revelation exclusively in terms of its first-century settings. *Futurists* see John's visions primarily coming to fruition in the end times. *Historicists* believe it is a book meant to describe history from John's time in Patmos to the end times. *Idealists* view Revelation as a symbolic story of timeless truths, especially of good conquering evil.

673. "Apocalyptic" writing is very symbolic. As a result, it is important that readers understand Revelation as a distinct book of the Bible. To understand what is being said, readers must recognize symbols: stars are angels, "the great prostitute" is Babylon (possibly Rome?), lampstands are churches, and the heavenly Jerusalem is the wife of the Lamb, Christ.

674. A unique feature of Revelation is the frequent use of the number *seven*. This happens fifty-two times! The number seven is a symbol for completeness; there are references to the seven churches, seven seals, seven signs, seven crowns, and many other items numbering seven.

675. The extraordinary prophetic vision of the second coming of Jesus and the last judgment were given while John was exiled on Patmos, an Aegean island, used as a Roman penal colony. The author had been banished there for his preaching most likely during the reign of Roman emperor Domitian (A.D. 81–96).

676. Apocalypse is the Greek name for the Book of Revelation. The word literally means "to unveil" or "to reveal something that has been hidden." The early church had numerous books claiming to reveal future events, and it wasn't until the fourth century that John's apocalypse was recognized as the one inspired version.

677. John heard a voice telling him what to do before he viewed the speaker (1:10–12). The voice told John to write down what he saw and then to send it to the seven churches. When John turned around, he viewed "someone 'like a son of man'" speaking to him. The person, Jesus Christ, is described as having hair that was white like wool and even snow, with eyes blazing fire. The speaker was dressed in a robe with a gold sash around his chest.

678. John was given direct instruction as to whom to address his account: the seven churches in Ephesus, Smyrna, Pergamum, Thyatira, Sardis, Philadelphia, and Laodicea. Each of the seven receives individual instructions tailored to their particular problems and weaknesses.

679. The pattern for these individual instructions is generally the same for all seven churches: commendation for their current efforts, expressions of disappointment for weakness or sin, and straightforward direction on how to correct the situation.

680. The churches are chastised and warned for forgetting to show love to Christ and one another, for failing to stand strong in the face of persecution, for allowing dissidents and religious heresy to exist in their churches, for being "dead" in their faith and refusing to repent, and for being lukewarm in their faith and not taking a solid stance within their surroundings.

681. Interestingly, all seven churches are given a promise if they will "overcome" the current situation. The promises all include being one with Christ through salvation, yet there is also mention of eternal reward, having authority over other nations, and being seated with Christ on his heavenly throne.

682. John discusses the throne in heaven where God sits. There is lightning, thunder, and great light. Brilliant color surrounds the Lord, his light reflected in gemlike beams. Surrounding the throne are twenty-four other smaller thrones with an elder seated in each one. The elders are in a constant state of worship of the Almighty.

683. The four living creatures behind the throne are truly monstrous visions. They too worship the Lord. They are covered with eyes, in order to see every detail. They each have six wings, though their images are all different—a figure like a lion, one like an ox, another with a face like a man, and the last resembling an eagle. Their job is to guard the heavenly throne as well as lead the others in worship. Revelation says that "day and night they never stop saying: 'Holy, holy, holy is the Lord God Almighty, who was, and is, and is to come'" (4:8).

684. A scroll bearing seven seals is held by Christ, but there is no one worthy to open it anywhere on earth. John says he weeps at the sight because he desperately wants to see what the scroll has to say. Yet there is one worthy to open the scroll. A Lamb that was slain appears, bearing seven horns and seven eyes (symbols of the seven spirits God had sent out into all the earth [5:6]). The lamb is a symbol of Christ—the righteous figure who was the atoning sacrifice for all people.

685. The Lamb is the only figure worthy to open the scroll. All in heaven fall down to worship him. It is undeniable that God and the Lamb are the Father and the Son and deserve equal reverence and awe.

686. As the Lamb opens the seals, many terrible things happen on earth. John speaks openly, understanding that such things are inescapable for those who have not turned to the Lamb in repentance. Each seal represents a source of destructive power that is unleashed on the earth. The fourth seal unleashes Death and Hades, who are given power over one quarter of the earth to kill, whether with a sword, by famine and plague, or with wild beasts (6:8).

687. Mention is made of the 144,000 believers who are sealed. Though Revelation says they were from the twelve tribes of Israel (7:4), it is uncertain if this is a symbolic number of those who withstood the last days of tribulation as Christians. Whoever they are, they are given seals on their foreheads to claim them as Christ's own so they are not harmed.

688. Those who have believed are sealed in the Lamb and joyfully present in heaven. John says they were dressed in white robes and were waving palm branches and praising God and the Lamb. Their numbers are too great to count, according to John, and they are from every corner of the earth and speak every tongue imaginable.

689. Those remaining on earth are tortured violently for five months by plagues, natural disasters, and warfare. Revelation 9: 6 says, "During those days men will seek death, but will not find it; they will long to die, but death will elude them." It is a terrible picture, and though there will be a third of mankind who will die, the remaining people will still be unrepentant. The Bible states that this is the period of the first woe, and that two more will follow, correlating to the angels blowing their trumpets.

690. Two witnesses are mentioned in Revelation 11. It is unknown exactly who these two figures are. It is believed they are modeled after Moses and Elijah, two major prophets of the Old Testament. However, it is possible that these are actual believers who testify in the last days before the return of Christ. Another possibility is that these two witnesses will suffer martyrdom for their testimony. In any case, they are eventually overcome by a beast, and their deaths are heralded as a victory for those still on earth. But God will raise the two witnesses, and they will come to heaven.

691. A terrible earthquake occurs after the witnesses are raised. Revelation 11:13 says seven thousand people are killed. The survivors are terrified and recognize that this is Christ acting against them. They are terrified and yet do not repent. This is the end of the second woe.

692. The turning point of the Book of Revelation comes in chapter 11. It is loudly proclaimed that the kingdom is Christ's, and he will reign forever. Yet the war is not over between good and evil. A battle is to be waged in heaven. Chapter 12 opens with a woman giving birth in heaven, and all eagerly looking on at this wondrous sign—she will birth the Messiah. But then a red dragon appears, and he tries to eat her child. However, he is not successful. The male infant is brought to God, who is on his throne. The woman is taken to a place of spiritual protection for a period of 1,260 days.

693. A battle is then waged in heaven. Christ's angels, who are led by Michael, and the devil (the red dragon) and his angels wage a brutal war. The dragon is not strong enough to succeed. Satan is thrown to earth with his angels following. The dragon is so enraged at his loss that he goes after the woman who birthed the Messiah.

694. The devil is unsuccessful in his pursuit of the woman, so he turns to her children who remain on earth: those who love and obey God. He is determined to kill them all or turn them from their God. He calls upon a beast to help him.

695. This beast, though he is powerful, has a limited amount of time to reign: forty-two months. This beast comes out of the sea and is given all the power that Satan has. He will take over the earth, subject God's people to tyranny, and gather the worship of all those who are not signed and sealed with Christ's blood. Most consider this figure to be the true and final antichrist.

696. Interestingly, forty-two months is considered a symbolic length of time—three-and-a-half-years. The period of forty-two months is also mentioned in Revelation 11:2. Many people believe the premise for this belief comes from a time when Jews were suffering persecution under Antiochus Epiphanes around 175 B.C. Others say this is a natural division of the number seven into two equal parts, each being equally good and evil.

697. Another beast emerges from the earth. This beast makes everyone on earth worship the antichrist. This beast has great power and is able to kill all who do not worship the antichrist. The earthly beast's greater claim to fame, however, is that he forces everyone to have a mark on his or her forehead or right hand. Those who refuse the mark are not allowed to buy or sell anything from anyone and will presumably suffer greatly. The beast is known by his number: 666.

698. The identity and meaning of the mystical beast numbered 666 has deeply concerned Christians throughout history. Its symbolism has been assigned to Satanism in popular culture and to such notorious figures as Napoleon and Hitler. Some scholars believe that while Satan is a major player in Revelation, the meaning of 666 was clear to the people of the time of its writing. In both Greek and Hebrew, letters doubled as numerals.

699. One solution to the 666 puzzle. The number is produced by adding up the Hebrew letters of "Kaisar Neron," or Emperor Nero, which reaches an equivalent of the number 666. Other possibilities have been other persecuting leaders, such as Euanthas and Lateinos. Still others believe 666 is significant as a symbol of triune evil, as each of the three digits are one number short of the perfect number seven.

700. Those who have the mark of the beast suffer great misery in the end times. The beast is felled and they are left on their own. Seven plagues are waged on them by seven different angels. These plagues are also referred to as the "seven bowls of God's wrath." Through these dreadful days, the people still refuse to repent. They curse God and continue to follow the beast.

701. Kings are gathered from all corners of the world to gather at the place called Armageddon (a Hebrew word), presumably for the final battle. John then sees a vision of a woman riding a beast—Babylon is her name; the beast is the antichrist. Babylon will fall, much to the fear and sadness of those people who associated with her. Those with the mark of the beast had worshiped her, even adored her.

702. God's army will do battle under the leadership of a rider on a white horse. Revelation 19:13 says, "his name is the Word of God." The rider leads victoriously forward, and eventually the beast and his false prophet (presumed to be the beast numbered 666) are cast into the fiery lake of sulfur.

703. Satan is then bound for a thousand years. He will be allowed out for a time following this period, according to Revelation 20. Those who suffered during the reign of the beast as Christians and did not succumb and did not receive the beast's mark are raised and seated with Christ for the thousand-year time period. This is called the first resurrection, since only those recently killed are raised from the dead; the rest will wait until the final resurrection.

704. The final judgment is covered in Revelation 20. God sits on his throne with the Book of Life and judges all who have died. All the dead, from the earth and the sea and Hades, are judged by what they had done (v. 12). All whose names are not in the book are thrown into the lake of fire, as are death and Hades.

705. God proclaims the old order completed and promises an end to "death or mourning or crying or pain" (Rev. 21:4). Everything will be new, perfect, and forever, because God has conquered death and Christ has vanquished sin.

706. The New Jerusalem, according to some interpreters, is another name for the holy city and has a mixture of elements from Jerusalem, the temple, and the Garden of Eden. John describes in vivid detail its gold and precious stones, and the beauty of this holy place. He even measures the city with a gold measuring rod! Others believe this term is a metaphorical allusion to heaven in general, connoting the place where God and his people reside in holy communion.

Part III

Putting It All Together

19

The Trinity Triangle

707. The doctrine of the Trinity is more clearly defined in the New Testament than in the Old. Several times the three persons of the Trinity are shown together and seemingly are equal to one another. At the baptism of Jesus, the Spirit descended on him and a voice from God out of heaven identified Jesus as his beloved Son (Matt. 3:16–17). Jesus prayed that the Father would send another Comforter (John 14:16). The disciples were told to baptize in the name (singular) of the Father, Son, and the Holy Spirit (Matt. 28:19). The three persons of the Trinity are also associated together in their work (1 Cor. 12:4–6; Eph. 1:3–14; 1 Peter 1:2; 3:18; Rev. 1:4–6).

708. The fact of the Trinity is taught in the Old Testament. The very name for God is *Elohim*—a plural word. Plural pronouns were often used for God (see Gen. 1:26), and even the Hebrew word used to refer to "one God" was the word *echad,* which connotes a compound unity. There are also references to both "the Son" and "the Spirit of God" throughout the Old Testament, clearly referring to the Trinity.

709. The Trinity of God. Though the term *trinity* does not occur in the Bible, it had very early usage in the church. Its Greek form, *trias,* seems to have been first used by Theophilus of Antioch (A.D. 181), and its Latin form, *trinitas,* by Tertullian (A.D. 220). In Christian theology, the term *Trinity* means that there are three eternal distinctions in the one divine essence, known respectively as Father, Son, and Holy Spirit. These three distinctions are three persons, and one may speak of the tri-personality of God. The doctrine of the Trinity *is* a great mystery. However, it was not birthed by speculation, but was given as revelation in Scripture.

710. "You deserted the Rock, who fathered you; you forgot the God who gave you birth" (Deut. 32:18). Not only is God the father of Jesus Christ, God is our father and our creator.

711. "Jesus said, 'Do not hold on to me, for I have not yet returned to the Father. Go instead to my brothers and tell them, "I am returning to my Father and your Father, to my God and your God"'" (John 20:17). After Christ's resurrection, he appeared to Mary Magdalene. His instructions to her demonstrate God is fully heavenly Father and God to both himself and to all who believe.

712. "For to us a child is born, to us a son is given, and the government will be on his shoulders. And he will be called Wonderful Counselor, Mighty God, Everlasting Father, Prince of Peace" (Isa. 9:6). The prophet Isaiah's words remained a testimony to God's people of the promised Messiah throughout many generations. That the people believed a Messiah would come is unquestionable. However, they were looking for an earthly king who would bring Israel to great heights rather than a Savior who would redeem the world and be their heavenly King first.

713. "As Jesus was coming up out of the water, he saw heaven being torn open and the Spirit descending on him like a dove. And a voice came from heaven: 'You are my Son, whom I love; with you I am well pleased'" (Mark 1:10–11). God himself, visible through the person of the Holy Spirit, spoke to Jesus as John the Baptist baptized Jesus in the Jordan River.

714. "Now the earth was formless and empty, darkness was over the surface of the deep, and the Spirit of God was hovering over the waters" (Gen. 1:2). The Spirit was present at the creation of the world and remains just as present today.

715. "But you will receive power when the Holy Spirit comes on you; and you will be my witnesses in Jerusalem, and in all Judea and Samaria, and to the ends of the earth" (Acts 1:8). Jesus made this promise to his disciples before ascending into heaven. The Book of Acts studies the early church; chapter 2 tells of the Holy Spirit's coming at Pentecost.

716. Trinitarian belief as expressed by the Athanasian Creed. "We worship one God in the Trinity, and the Trinity in unity; we distinguish among the persons, but we do not divide the substance." It goes on to say, "The entire three persons are co-eternal and coequal with one another. . . ." "The heart of Christian faith in God is the revealed mystery of the Trinity. *Trinitas* is a Latin word meaning three-ness. Christianity rests on the doctrinal truths of the *trinitas,* the tri-personality, of God. Each person in the Godhead played not only a significant role in our creation but also our redemption."—J. I. Packer

717. Perfect harmony. The persons of the Godhead relate one to another in perfect harmony and intimacy—a perfect society. One theologian explains, "If there were no trinity, there could be no incarnation, no objective redemption, and therefore no salvation; for there would be no one capable of acting as mediator between God and man." The Trinity allows for eternal love. Love was before creation, yet love needs an object. Love is always flowing among the persons of the Trinity.

718. The three persons of the Trinity act in cooperation with one another. No one person in the Godhead acts free of the connection of the other two. They are anchored—the Spirit and Son do not act in opposition to the Father. Were they to do so, we could not speak of the Trinity as "one God, with three distinct persons."

719. The Father is "the God of Peace," the Son is "our Peace," and the Holy Spirit is "the Spirit of Peace" and produces "the fruit of . . . peace." Peace expresses the deepest desire and need of the human heart. It represents the greatest measure of contentment and satisfaction in life.

720. There are seven different views on the makeup of the Trinity in regards to subordination and equality between the three distinct persons of the Godhead. Some of these views place more emphasis on power and "line of command" than others; all respect and revere the Trinity as biblical and historically faithful to the beliefs of the church.

721. The first model posits both the Son and the Spirit proceeding from the Father. The Son and Spirit are on the same level yet independent of one another. The Father is the source of the latter two, yet all three are equally God.

722. Another model states that the Father again is the beginning point from which the Son proceeds. The Spirit, however, proceeds from both the Father and the Son. The Spirit does not have any impact, in essence, on the other two.

723. A third model places the Father and the Son on an equal plane, making them equal in glory. However, the Spirit proceeds from the two at a lower level, acting as a mediator between the divine Father and Son and the earthly world below.

724. Another model shows less of a triangle effect and instead posits that all things originate with the Father, are then passed to the Son, and then through the Son to the Holy Spirit. The Father, Son, and Holy Spirit are all on the same plane of deity, but all things originate with the Father. This view is deeply rooted in both the Eastern and Western churches.

725. The fifth model comes from a more mystical view within the church. The Father is the head, and the rest—the Son, Spirit, and the world—emanate from him. However, the model also holds a place for a return to the Father. It is believed that the Spirit prepares the world for the Son, and the Son (along with the Holy Spirit) leads us back to the Father. This model definitely loses the equality of all three persons within the Godhead.

726. Augustine's model represents a much more fluid relationship between the three persons of the Godhead. The Father, Son, and Spirit are all on the same level (negating a triangle view such as models one and two), but the Spirit is actually in between the Father and the Son. The Spirit proceeds from the Father and the Son. David N. Bell suggests the relationship is similar to that of the workings of an electric battery where the Father is the "positive" and the Son is the "negative"—the Spirit is "the current flowing and flashing between them." He goes on to explain that there is only one substance, one current, but the battery will not function without both the positive and negative ends as well as a route for the current between them. A weakness of this view is that it tends to put the Spirit in a subordinate role as a conduit of the currents flowing from Father to Son and vice versa.

727. The seventh and final model takes more of a give-and-take approach between the three persons. Father, Son, and Spirit are points on a circle with no end and no beginning. As the Father influences the Son, the Son influences the Spirit, and the Spirit influences the Father. It is less a picture of two or one being subordinate to the other and more a picture of interdependence between all three. Though the Father might be the starting point from which the Son and Spirit proceed, the Son and Spirit proceed *to* the Father with their own response.

728. Various analogies have been made in order to explain the mystery of the Trinity. Augustine proposed that the three persons may be likened to "proposed lover, beloved, and love itself." Another is that of the components of an apple: the core, flesh, and peel representing God, the Son, and the Holy Spirit as the "visible," "tangible" peel that wraps the flesh of the Son and the core of the Father into one thing, an apple.

729. Tertullian and Anselm, both church fathers, had views with a more subordinationist approach. Tertullian likened the persons of the Trinity to the root, tree, and fruit. Anselm offered a picture of a spring, stream, and lake to demonstrate how the Trinity flowed and existed.

730. Others prefer to speak of the Trinity in more equal terms. For example, one space with three dimensions: height, length, and depth. Or the three phases of matter: solid, liquid, and gas. All may exist at the same time, with the temperature being the determining factor.

731. The Nicene Creed is a statement of the orthodox faith of the early Christian church. Written in response to heresies that included the doctrine of the Trinity, among others, its words remain a testimony of the church's belief in this respect. The creed was used by both Western and Eastern churches, although the Western church insisted on the inclusion of the phrase "and the Son" (known as the *Filioque*) in the article on the procession of the Holy Spirit. The Eastern church remains steadfast in leaving this phrase out. The creed covers the three persons of the Trinity separately.

732. "I believe in one God, the Father Almighty, Maker of heaven and earth, and of all things visible and invisible."—Nicene Creed, First Article

733. "And in one Lord Jesus Christ, the only-begotten Son of God, begotten of the Father before all worlds; God of God, Light of Light, very God of very God; begotten, not made, being of one substance with the Father, by whom all things were made."—Nicene Creed, Second Article

734. "And I believe in the Holy Spirit, the Lord and Giver of life; who proceedeth from the Father and the Son; who with the Father and the Son together is worshipped and glorified; who spoke by the prophets."—Nicene Creed, Fourth Article

735. Denial of the Trinity leads to dangerous theology. Without a view of an active, dynamic God who performs as the Trinity does, it's easy to fall into heresy—deism, pantheism, and agnosticism to name a few. Deism views God as one who is unattached and uninvolved, a God who put the world in motion but doesn't monitor it. Pantheism believes God is inseparable from the world, and many parts of the world are worshiped as God. In agnosticism, God cannot be known—he is a mystery that is impossible to even know. When the Trinity is denied, often Christ's deity is questioned, and the story of the Bible, God's Word, is in effect lost.

20

The Names of the Members of the Trinity

THE NAMES OF GOD THE FATHER

736. The names of God in Scripture describe his character . . .

a faithful God who does no wrong
a forgiving God

God of grace
God of hope
God of love and peace
God of peace
a jealous and avenging God

737. The names of God describe him as our protector . . .

a refuge for his people
a refuge for the needy in his distress
a refuge for the oppressed
a refuge for the poor
a sanctuary
a shade from the heat
a shelter from the storm
a stronghold in times of trouble
a fortress of salvation
an ever-present help in trouble
defender of widows
our dwelling place

738. God's names reveal his leadership . . .

a Master in heaven
commander of the Lord's army
God our strength
helper of the fatherless
the great King above all gods
the only God
the just and mighty One Shepherd

739. God's name reveals his royalty . . .

a glorious crown
a source of strength
eternal King

God of Glory
Most High
the Exalted God
Sovereign Lord
the Glorious Father
the Majestic Glory
the Majesty in heaven
your glory
your praise
the Glory of Israel
God of gods

740. The names of God reveal his creativity . . .

architect and builder
builder of everything
Creator of heaven and earth
he who reveals his thoughts to man
the potter
the gardener (husbandman)
only wise God
him who is able to do immeasurably more than all we ask or
   imagine

741. His names reveal his fatherhood . . .

Father
Father of compassion
Father of our spirits
Father of the heavenly lights
Father to the fatherless
God and Father of our Lord Jesus Christ
God of Abraham, Isaac, and Jacob
God of all mankind
God our Father

742. The names of God reveal his majesty . . .

God
God of the Sabbath *(El Sabaoth)*
God Almighty *(El Shaddai)*
God Most High
God my Maker
King of Glory
God over all the kingdoms of the earth
King of heaven

743. God's names reveal his strength . . .

God my rock
God my Savior
God my stronghold
one to be feared
he who raised Christ from the dead
him who is able to keep you from falling
Lord who strikes the blow
our Mighty One
the one who sustains me
the strength of my heart
the rock in whom I take refuge
Rock of our salvation
our refuge and strength

744. His names reveal his actions on our behalf . . .

God of all comfort
God of retribution
God who avenges me
God who gives endurance and encouragement
God who relents from sending calamity
he who blots out your transgressions
he who comforts you

745. The names of God reveal his greatness . . .

great and awesome God
great and powerful God
great, mighty, and awesome God
Lord will provide
the Almighty
the consuming fire
the everlasting God
your very great reward

746. His names reveal his nature . . .

God of truth
living and true God
jealous
the spring of living water
love
you who keep your covenant of love with your servants
you who love the people
the faithful God
the God who saves me
you who hear prayer
the Eternal God

747. His names reveal his eternity . . .

I Am
the living Father
God of the living

748. The names of God reveal his judgeship . . .

Judge of all the earth
him who is ready to judge the living and the dead
our judge
our lawgiver

the true God
you who judge righteously and test the heart and mind
Righteous Father
the compassionate and gracious God
Righteous Judge
our redeemer

749. The names of God reveal his holiness . . .

Holy Father
Holy One
Holy One among you
Lord who makes you holy

750. His names reveal his lordship . . .

Adonai (Lord)
Lord Almighty
Lord God
Lord our Peace
Lord (Jehovah)
Lord Most High
Lord my Banner
Lord my Rock
Lord of all the earth
Lord of heaven and earth
Lord of lords
Lord our God
Lord our Maker
Lord our shield
Lord who heals you
Lord who is there

751. His names reveal that he is our Maker . . .

God our Maker
Maker of all things
Maker of heaven and earth

he who forms the hearts of all
the God who sees me
the God of the spirits of all mankind

752. The names of God reveal that he is personal . . .

my advocate
my comforter in sorrow
my confidence
my help
my helper
my hiding place
my hope
my light
my mighty rock
my refuge in the day of disaster
my refuge in times of trouble
my song
my strong deliverer
my support

THE NAMES OF GOD THE SON

753. Jesus is the Son . . .

Branch of the Lord
Son of Mary
Heir of Salvation
Son of the Living God
heir of all things
his one and only Son
Son of the Most High God
Holy One of God
Lion of the Tribe of Judah
Son of the Blessed One

754. Jesus is Eternal . . .

Emmanuel (God with us)
Eternal Life
the Beginning and the End
the Amen
the First and the Last
the last Adam
the Living One
the Living Stone

755. Jesus is the Messiah . . .

Christ
Anointed One
Bread of Life
Hope of Glory
Horn of Salvation
one who makes men holy
one who speaks to the Father in our defense
Passover Lamb
Prince of Peace
Redeemer
the man from heaven
Savior of the world
the stone the builders rejected

756. Christ's character is revealed in his names . . .

Lord
our hope
faithful and true
our peace
fragrant offering and sacrifice to God
our righteousness, holiness, and redemption
Great Physician

Righteous Judge
sure foundation

757. Christ's actions are revealed in his names . . .

author and perfecter of our faith
author of our salvation
Bridegroom
chief cornerstone
consolation of Israel
friend of tax collectors and sinners
covenant for the people
he who comes down from heaven and gives life to the world
he who searches hearts and minds
him who died and came to life again
him who loves us and has freed us from our sins
Lamb of God
mediator of a new covenant

758. Christ's humanity is revealed in his names . . .

the Son of Man
firstborn among the dead
a Nazarene
firstborn over all creation
Man of sorrows
Root of David
the Son

759. Christ's divinity is revealed in his names . . .

Alpha and Omega
Ancient of Days
author of life
God of all the earth
Son of God

Light
image of the invisible God
Immanuel (God with us)
Judge of the living and the dead
Messiah
our God and Savior Jesus Christ
Sovereign and Lord
Word of God

760. The priesthood of Jesus is revealed in his names . . .

apostle and high priest
Great High Priest
merciful and faithful high priest
Rabbi
Teacher
the Head
the atoning sacrifice for our sins
Servant

761. Christ's beauty is revealed in his names . . .

Beloved
Holy and Righteous One
Rose of Sharon
the Lord our Righteousness
Fountain
True Vine
Shiloh

762. Christ's majesty and kingship are revealed in his names . . .

blessed and only Ruler
Bright and Morning Star
chosen and precious cornerstone

Crown of Splendor
Desire of Nations
Master
head of every man
head of the body, the church
head over every power and authority
King of Kings
King of the ages
King of the Jews
Ruler over the nations
Ruler of God's creation
Ruler of the kings of the earth

763. The protection of Christ is revealed in his names . . .

a banner for the peoples
Deliverer
Good Shepherd
ransom for all men
Shepherd and Overseer of your souls
the gate (door)
Refiner and Purifier
Great Shepherd of the sheep

764. The lordship of Jesus is revealed in his names . . .

Lord (Kurios)
Lord and Savior Jesus Christ
Lord of Glory
Lord of lords
Lord of peace
Lord of the harvest
Lord of the Sabbath
Lord (Rabboni)

765. The illumination of Jesus is revealed in his names . . .

Light of Life
Light of Men

Light of the World
Light of the Gentiles
Morning Star
the true light
the radiance of God's glory
the truth

766. The blessing of Jesus is revealed in his names . . .

indescribable gift
Dayspring
guarantee of a better covenant
Resurrection and the Life
Wonderful Counselor
the Bright and Morning Star

THE NAMES OF GOD THE HOLY SPIRIT

767. The names for the Spirit reveal his actions . . .

Counselor
a deposit guaranteeing what is to come
Spirit of judgment
Spirit of life
Spirit of sonship (adoption)
the gift

768. The names for the Spirit reveal his character . . .

Breath of the Almighty
Spirit of counsel and of power
Spirit of grace and supplication
Spirit of holiness
Spirit of truth
Spirit of justice
Spirit of wisdom and of understanding

Spirit of wisdom and revelation
Spirit of faith
Spirit of fire

769. The names for the Spirit reveal his divinity . . .

Holy Spirit
Holy One
Spirit of Christ
Spirit of the living God
Spirit of the Lord
Spirit of the Sovereign Lord
Voice of the Lord

770. The names for the Spirit reveal his greatness . . .

Spirit of God
the promised Holy Spirit
Spirit of Glory
God's seal

21

A Heavenly Father

771. The Father is recognized as God. A brief scan of the New Testament reveals the numerous times and roles in which the Father is identified as God. "Paul, an apostle—not from men nor through man, but through Jesus Christ and God the Father, who raised him from the dead" (Gal. 1:1 NRSV; see also John 6:27; Rom. 1:7).

772. Father—a distinguishing title of the New Testament. To Israel, he was revealed as *Jehovah,* and the patriarchs reveled in such triumphant names as *God Almighty* and *Lord of Heaven and Earth.* But in all the divine names or titles disclosed in Scripture, there is no revelation of the fatherhood of God until his beloved

Son taught his disciples to pray, "Our Father which art in heaven, Hallowed be thy name" (Matt. 6:9).

773. Old Testament references to the Father are figurative. Only a few references to God's fatherhood are mentioned in Old Testament Scriptures and they are mainly figurative and used as illustrations. "Like as a father pitieth his children, so the LORD pitieth them that fear him" (Ps. 103:13). It is in this way that he also likens himself to a mother. "As one whom his mother comforteth, so will I comfort you" (Isa. 66:13).

774. God reserved his role of Father. We see glimpses of God's relationship to his redeemed people as in the song of Moses where we find the question, "Is not he thy father that hath bought thee?" (Deut. 32:6). He also speaks of himself as "Israel's Father" in Jeremiah (31:9) and refers to Israel as his "firstborn" (Exod. 4:22; Hosea 11:1). But scholars hold that God reserved his role of Father to express his unique relationship founded only on the accomplished redemption of the coming Messiah. Jesus said, "No man cometh unto the Father, *but by me*" (John 14:6 KJV, emphasis added).

775. A tender name. Of all the divine names, none is more full of comfort or more touching to the heart than that of *Father*. In the Gospels alone, we find that Matthew mentions "the Father" 44 times; Mark, 5 times; Luke, 17 times; and John, 122 times. John's is especially the Gospel revealing the Father, and a definite aspect of God's role is emphasized in each chapter where this name is mentioned.

776. Aspects of Father. The identifying terms used by the Son of God in the New Testament Scriptures are: *the Father, Father, my Father, your Father, our Father, Holy Father, Righteous Father, Abba Father.* Added to these are several relative expressions in the epistles that, along with those found in the Gospels, emphasize the many-sided character inherent in the fatherhood of God:

- a Father
- God the Father
- God our Father
- God and Father of our Lord Jesus Christ
- Father of mercies

- Father of spirits
- Father of lights
- Father of glory

777. "**Jesus said to them, 'If God were your Father,** you would love me, for I came from God and now am here. I have not come on my own; but he sent me'" (John 8:42). God is the Father of those who believe in him; he is the Creator of all, but the Father of the elect.

778. "**'You do not know me or my Father,' Jesus replied.** 'If you knew me, you would know my Father also'" (John 8:19). The Father cannot be known unless it is through the Son. You cannot know the one without the other.

779. "**If you [believers] then,** though you are evil, know how to give good gifts to your children, how much more will your Father in heaven give the Holy Spirit to those who ask him!" (Luke 11:13). The heavenly Father's greatest gift to his redeemed people who have experienced Christ's atonement is the Holy Spirit.

780. *The* **Father.** As *the* is emphasized in this title, God's own personal glory as Father is conveyed wherever it is used. The exclusiveness of his being and behavior as our heavenly Father is prominent here. In the Gospel of John, this title is used several times to illustrate the Father as the one above all other fathers, as the source of all things. "He that hath seen me hath seen the Father" (John 14:9 KJV; see also 1:14; 3:35; 4:21; 6:44; 12:49; 14:24; 14:26; 16:27).

781. Father. While Jesus often spoke about God, he only addressed him once as such: "My God, my God" (Matt. 27:46). Apart from this exception, Christ addressed him as Father—the single most intimate term for the relationship existing between the Father and the Son. His first recorded use of *Father* was when at age twelve Jesus spoke to Joseph and Mary about being in the temple (Luke 2:49). And the last occasion was on the cross, where his final prayer was, "Father, into your hands I commit my spirit" (Luke 23:46).

782. The mystery of the incarnation is that Jesus was "conceived of the Holy Spirit, and born of the virgin Mary." He came as the son of man, but not as *a* son of man. Though he was foster parented by Joseph, he was God's only begotten Son. He had only one Father.

783. *My* Father. Spoken only by Jesus, the pronoun of personal possession—*my*—expresses not only an eternal relationship between him and God the Father, but also in the fellowship of mutual love and action on behalf of the believers. "Neither shall any man pluck them out of my hand. . . . No man is able to pluck them out of my Father's hand. I and my Father are one" (John 10:28–30).

784. *Your* Father. Fourteen times in Matthew's Gospel alone does this particular combination occur, bringing with it responsibility to the Lord and to others. The privilege of being God's children through the finished work of Christ brings a certain obligation. "Let your light so shine before men, that they may see your good works, and glorify *your Father* which is in heaven" (5:16 KJV, emphasis added).

785. *Our* Father. In response to the request of his disciples, "Lord, teach us to pray," Jesus guided them with a model to follow, opening with "*Our Father* which art in heaven" (Matt. 6:9 KJV, emphasis added). But this was not the language of Jesus *and* his disciples, meaning joint relationship. This prayer was intended for the family of the redeemed rather than a prayer that Jesus himself prayed. Why? Jesus had no evil to be delivered from and no trespasses to be forgiven.

786. *Holy* Father. In the prayer recorded in John 17, Jesus used the title of Father different ways. First, he repeated the single name, *Father,* four times (vv. 1, 5, 21, 24), while speaking to God about his past glory, present life, approaching sacrifice, and future glory. But in verse 9, he begins to pray for the believers, "I pray not for the world, but for them which thou hast given me; for they are thine" (KJV). His burden was that his redeemed ones might be kept from evil in the world. He interceded for their sanctification, so the term *Holy Father* was most fitting.

787. *Righteous* Father. Why did Jesus use "Righteous Father" in John 17:25 and not "Holy Father"? In the last verse of this most remarkable prayer, Jesus said, "I have declared unto them thy name, and will declare it" (17:26). With his approaching death,

Jesus knew divine righteousness would be manifested. Here he cries out to his Father who knows his ultimate purpose.

788. *Abba* Father. *Abba* is an Aramaic word that describes simple affection for the Father (Mark 14:36; Rom. 8:15; Gal. 4:6). In Jewish and old Christian prayers, it was a name by which God was addressed. *Abba* is the name a child would use and *Father* expresses an intelligent realization of the relationship. The two combined express the confident love and growing intelligence of a child.

22

The Son, a Savior

789. The Son is recognized as God. The doctrine of the deity of Christ is crucial to the Christian faith. "What think you of Christ?" is the paramount question of life (see Matt. 16:15; 22:42). Jesus Christ is the greatest of all men, but he is infinitely more than mere man. He is Immanuel, God with us. Matthew explicitly applies the passage from Isaiah 7:14 to Jesus (Matt. 1:22–23).

790. Jesus reflects God. Christ was moved at the sight of the straining, clueless crowds—but a millennium earlier it was written of Jehovah: "As a father has compassion on his children, so the LORD has compassion on those who fear him; for he knows how we are formed, he remembers that we are dust" (Ps. 103:13–14). We know Jesus took pity on orphans, but Hosea said of the Father, "In you the fatherless find compassion" (Hosea 14:3). Yes, Jesus wept at the tomb of Lazarus, but of the Father we learn, "Precious in the sight of the LORD is the death of his saints" (Ps. 116:15).

791. The "Angel of the Lord" is a recurring phrase in the Old Testament and has special reference to the preincarnate second person of the Trinity. His appearances in the Old Testament foreshadowed his coming in the flesh. The Angel of the Lord is identified with the Lord and yet distinguished from him. He appeared to Hagar, Abraham, Jacob, Moses, Israel, Balaam, Gideon, Manoah, Elijah, and David. The Angel of the Lord slew 185,000 Assyrians, stood among the myrtle trees in Zechariah's vision, defended Joshua the high priest against Satan, and was one of the three men who appeared to Abraham.

792. The Christmas story reveals the depth of God's love to us. Matthew's and Luke's Gospels tell the story of the virgin birth, the humble beginnings of Jesus, and the joyous celebration set off in heaven when Christ was born. Though missed by many, God allowed both great (the magi) and humble (the shepherds) to join in the celebration.

793. The baby Jesus was like any other baby—he was human and had the same needs as babies do today. He cried to be held and fed, needed his diapers changed, and learned to talk as any other baby does.

794. Jesus did not receive his name, which means "the Messiah" or "the Christ," until his eighth day when he was circumcised. The name had been given to Mary by the angel before she conceived, but the practice was to officially name the child when he was circumcised.

795. At twelve years of age, Jesus already demonstrated that he was aware of his life work. His parents had taken him to the Passover feast in Jerusalem. When they left, they thought he was with them, but he had stayed behind in order to speak with the teachers at the temple.

796. His ministry began when he was in his late twenties. John the Baptist was serving as a "voice in the wilderness" and calling the people to remember that their Savior was coming, that the time had come to repent.

797. The demons never failed to recognize Jesus as the "holy one of God" or "son of the Most High"; only human beings questioned his identity.

798. The Lord's preaching took him all over the area for three years. He traveled throughout Galilee, Judea, and Samaria. He healed the sick and brought hope to many through miracles. He often spoke in parables to the people to help them better understand what his ministry was all about.

799. Jesus spent much of his ministry life in and around the Sea of Galilee. Galileans in Bible times were considered country hicks by the more cosmopolitan residents of Jerusalem. Jesus spoke primarily to the humble people who labored on the land and were familiar with the animals and plants around them. His parables are filled with images of the natural world.

800. To the devout Jews who accepted Jesus, he was the promised Savior who fulfilled the promise expressed in their Scriptures of a coming "Messiah" or "anointed one" from the line of David who would deliver the Children of Israel and usher in a new age of peace under God's rule. Though he was later called the "Christ," this is not a name but a title. *Christos* comes from the Greek meaning "anointed one" or "Messiah."

801. As Christ rode a donkey into Jerusalem, he was hailed by the people with palm leaves and shouts of "Hosanna!" The people celebrated him as their king. They did not want the greatest gift that Christ offered and that they needed most. They wanted freedom from the Romans and a nation of their own instead, and thought that was what Christ brought, despite the many warnings and explanations given of his ministry.

802. Satan provoked Judas to betray Jesus, as it is stated in the Gospel of John. The treachery of Judas has provoked some speculation over motives, including the notion that he might have been an anti-Roman zealot who was disappointed that Jesus had not proved to be the rebel leader many were expecting. In Mark, Judas went to the chief priests to betray Jesus before being offered a bribe, suggesting that he had some other motive besides money. Matthew specifically states that Judas asked how much he would be given, and he was paid "thirty pieces of silver" in fulfillment of ancient Hebrew prophecy.

803. After the Last Supper, Jesus spent his last night of freedom in the Garden of Gethsemane on the slopes of the Mount of Olives. The name means "olive presses." In Jesus' time, the Mount of Olives was covered with a luxuriant growth of these trees, and the inhabitants of Jerusalem often rested there to seek relief from the sun.

804. "This day, even in this night, before the cock crows twice, you will deny me three times" (Mark 14:30). On the way to Gethsemane, Jesus told his disciple Peter this prophecy. The roosters first crowed about midnight, and they were so punctual that Roman soldiers used the sound as a signal for changing the guard. The roosters crowed a second time about three o'clock in the morning, which awakened the second watch of soldiers.

805. After Jesus was resurrected, he appeared several times to various disciples. His resurrection fulfilled every prophecy he and all the Old Testament prophets had made concerning the Savior of the world. Though some doubted, many believed and were brought to a saving understanding that Jesus was truly their Savior and the King of Kings.

23

A Spirit Was Sent

806. The study of the Holy Spirit is called "pneumatology," which comes from the Greek words *pneuma* (meaning "spirit") and *logos* (meaning "doctrine").

807. The Hebrew word that is commonly translated "Spirit" literally means "wind" or "breath." Thus the "Spirit of God" is literally the invisible, active presence of God. You can hear the wind and see its result as it moves the branches of a tree, but you cannot see the wind itself. Similarly the actions of the Holy Spirit are evident in the lives of believers, even though we cannot see him directly.

808. The Spirit is a person. Before it can be decided that the Holy Spirit is God, it must first be established that he is a person, not a mere influence or divine power. And he truly is. Though the Greek term for spirit is neuter, Jesus in John 14:26 and 16:13–14 used the masculine pronoun "he" when speaking of the Holy Spirit. He also has the three essential elements of personality: intellect (1 Cor. 2:11), sensibilities (Rom. 8:27; 15:30), and will (1 Cor. 12:11). He can be tempted (Acts 5:9), lied to (Acts 5:3), grieved (Eph. 4:30), resisted (Acts 7:51), insulted (Heb. 10:29), and blasphemed (Matt. 12:31–32).

809. The Holy Spirit is recognized as God. He is a divine person as can be shown by his attributes of deity: He is eternal (Heb. 9:14), omniscient (1 Cor. 2:10–11), omnipotent (Luke 1:35), and omnipresent (Ps. 139:7–10). Works of deity are also ascribed to him such as creation, regeneration, inspiration of the Scriptures, and raising of the dead.

810. Some groups (for example, the Jehovah's Witness cult) view the Holy Spirit as a "force" or "power," rather than as a person. However, that heresy grew largely from the translators of the King James Bible, who referred to the Spirit as "it."

811. The Holy Spirit has personality, as revealed by the fact that he has a will (1 Cor. 12:11), a mind (Rom. 8:27), knowledge (John 14:26), the ability to communicate (Acts 1:16), and emotions (Eph. 4:30). His personality is also demonstrated in the fact that he has a job: to teach, guide, restrain, comfort, and intercede on behalf of believers.

812. The New Testament reveals that the Spirit can be grieved, quenched, resisted, blasphemed, and insulted.

813. The Holy Spirit is referred to as "God" in Acts 5:3–4, as "Lord" in 2 Corinthians 3:18, and as being equal to the Father and the Son in Matthew 28:19.

814. Scripture reveals the divine attributes of the Holy Spirit, referring to him as eternal (Heb. 9:14), omniscient (John 14:26), omnipotent (Job 26:13), all wise (Isa. 40:13), sovereign (1 Cor. 12:11), and the giver of life (Rom. 8:2).

815. One of the most common descriptors for the Holy Spirit is the name "Comforter." This comes from the Greek word *paracletos*, which literally means "one who comes alongside." The Holy Spirit is God's way of personally coming alongside each believer (see John 15:26).

816. The Holy Spirit is referred to as our "guide" in several New Testament passages. This reveals the Spirit's job of leading believers into maturity in Christ. As John 16:13 puts it, "The Spirit of truth . . . will guide you . . ."

817. Romans 8:26–27 describes the Holy Spirit as our *intercessor*. In that role he will reveal the Father's will, pray with us, and connect us to the Father.

818. The work of the Holy Spirit is evident in creation (see Gen. 1:2, 26), in the inspiration of Scripture (see 2 Tim. 3:16 and 2 Peter 1:21), and in the salvation of humankind (see John 7:38–39).

819. The Holy Spirit was active in the Old Testament. He empowered Gideon in Judges 6:34, Samson in Judges 14:6, and David in 1 Samuel 16:13.

820. "Quenching the Spirit" is referred to in several passages of Scripture, including 1 Thessalonians 5:19, Psalm 51, and 1 Samuel 16:14. Sin, particularly secret sin in the life of a believer, will prevent the Spirit from working in one's life.

821. The Holy Spirit became manifest in the lives of believers on the day of Pentecost, when he came upon the members of the early church and allowed them to speak in other tongues so that everyone in the crowd heard their own language (see Acts 2).

822. "And be not drunk with wine . . . but be filled with the Spirit," Paul wrote in Ephesians 5:18. The "filling of the Spirit" is likened to being drunk, since control of our lives is turned over to something else—in this case, God. Some charismatic and Pentecostal groups believe this is a regular event in the lives of believers, while most other believers see the filling of the Spirit as a one-time event, occurring at the moment of salvation.

823. One of the activities of the Holy Spirit is to provide believers with spiritual gifts. Romans 12 and 1 Corinthians 12 both describe a number of gifts the Spirit gives to believers, including wisdom, knowledge, faith, healing, miracles, prophecy, tongues, interpretation, serving, teaching, discerning, and encouraging. While each believer has been given at least one spiritual gift, no one has a right to *ask* for a particular gift. These gifts blend together in a church to bring unity to the body of Christ.

824. The Holy Spirit also produces "fruit" in the lives of believers. Galatians 5:22–23 details some of the fruit that is produced: love, joy, peace, patience, kindness, goodness, faithfulness, gentleness, and self-control.

825. "Blasphemy against the Holy Spirit" is sometimes referred to as "the unpardonable sin." According to Matthew 12:22–32, Mark 3:22–30, and Luke 12:10, blasphemy against the Holy Spirit refers to examining the clear, supernatural work of God and ascribing it to Satan.

826. The Spirit was active all along from the beginning of time, hovering over the waters at creation and inspiring God's messengers throughout the Old Testament history—378 passages in the Hebrew Bible mention the Spirit.

24

The Word

827. The Bible is not only special revelation, but also the final authority on God. It is the embodiment of a divine revelation. The records containing this revelation are genuine, credible, and supernaturally inspired.

828. The Canon of Scripture is the supreme and only infallible source of theology. We do not forget the importance of reason, intuition, and the creeds and confessions of the church, but we understand these to be aids in the understanding of the revelation of God, particularly as contained in the Scriptures.

829. The Bible. Christians believe this book to be the true Word of God. From the creation account of Genesis to the end-time visions of Revelation, the story of Israel to Jesus' ministry, it is the source for what Christians believe and how they try to live.

830. The word *Bible* comes from the Greek word *biblia,* which means "books," which comes from another word, *byblos,* meaning papyrus, a material books were made from in ancient times.

831. The ancient Greeks obtained their supplies of paper from the port of Byblos, in what is now Lebanon. Their word for book—*biblion*—was derived from the name of this port, and from this we get our English word *Bible,* meaning the Book of books.

832. The word *Bible* **is not in the Bible.** The term came long after all the writings were completed and assembled.

833. The Bible is the world's best-selling book as well as the world's most shoplifted book!

834. The Bible is the most bought, yet least understood book. Nine out of ten Americans own a Bible, but fewer than half ever read it. Worldwide sales of the Bible are uncountable.

835. Just how big is the Bible? Stack ten average-sized nonfiction books printed today. That pile will contain the same number of words that are found in one Bible. That's close to one million words, not counting the number of words added—footnotes, verse numbers, concordances, etc.

836. The Bible looks like one book, but it is actually an anthology, a collection of many smaller books. In an even broader sense, it is not just an anthology of shorter works but an entire library.

837. Some Bible books are as short as half a page. One of the longest books—Jeremiah—is roughly the length of today's short novel. This makes the Bible's longest book a hundred times longer than its shortest book.

838. Though the Bible as a whole is much longer than nearly any other book we'd like to read, its individual books are mostly shorter than any other book we consider reading.

839. The Bible is an extraordinary gathering of many books of law, wisdom, poetry, philosophy, and history. The number of books in this portable library depends on which Bible you are holding. The Bible of a Jew is different from the Bible of a Roman Catholic, which in turn is different from the Bible of a Protestant.

840. The Bible is both ancient and contemporary as it deals with the unchanging issues of human existence: life, death, joy, sorrow, achievement, and failure. Yet these issues are couched in the language and correspondence of ancient times.

841. "The Bible is in my opinion the most sublime of all books; when all others will bore me, I will always go back to it with new pleasure; and when all human consolations will be lacking, never have I vainly turned to its own."—Jean Jacques Rousseau

842. "Testament" was another word for "covenant"—meaning an agreement, contract, or pact. For Christians, the Old Testament represents the ancient covenant made between God and his people. In the New Testament, Christians believe in a new covenant with God made through the life, death, and resurrection of Jesus.

843. Written over the course of a thousand years, primarily in ancient Hebrew, the Jewish Bible is the equivalent of Christianity's Old Testament. For Jews, there is no New Testament.

844. At least half as much time elapsed between the Bible's first book and its last (with well over a thousand years between the first writing and the time of the last), as has elapsed between its last book and now. This means that you can expect writing styles to vary not just between modern books and the Bible, but between the Bible books themselves.

845. The terms "Old Testament" and "New Testament" originated with the prophet Jeremiah. When he spoke about the glorious future for Israel that the prophets often spoke of, he said that God would "make a new covenant with the house of Israel." *Testament* means "covenant," and Jesus of Nazareth, the long-awaited Messiah, made a new covenant with God's people. The books of the New Testament provide the fulfillment of the promises made throughout the Old Testament books.

846. The translation of the Hebrew Scriptures into the *koine* Greek dialect was an outstanding literary accomplishment under the Ptolemies. This translation was called the *Septuagint*. The translation project is said to have been sponsored by Ptolemy II Philadelphus around the third century B.C. According to tradition, seventy-two Jewish scholars (six from each tribe) were summoned for the project. The work was finished in seventy-two days; the Jewish scholars were then sent away with many gifts.

847. The Septuagint provided a bridge between the thoughts and vocabulary of the Old and New Testaments. The language of the New Testament is not the *koine* of the everyday Greek, but the *koine* of the Jew living in Greek surroundings. By the New Testament era, it was the most widely used edition of the Old Testament.

848. Most Jews of Jesus' day spoke Aramaic, a Syrian language similar to Hebrew that was commonly used at the time. Jesus surely studied the formal Hebrew of the Torah, Prophets, and Writings. Whether he could also speak Greek is unknown. Jesus left no personal writings.

849. Both the Jewish Bible and Christian Old Testament contain the same thirty-nine books, although they are arranged and numbered in a slightly different order. In Jewish traditions, their Bible is called the *Tanakh*, an acronym of the Hebrew words *Torah* (for "law" or "teaching"), *Nevi'im* ("the Prophets"), and *Kethuvim* ("the Writings").

850. The Canon of Scripture is the complete and divine revelation of God, authoritative and binding in relation to the Christian faith and its practice. Since the Canon was closed (that is, all the inspired books were written for our edification), no books are to be added to it or taken away from it.

851. The word *canon* is an English version of the Greek word *kanon*, which in turn was borrowed from the Hebrew word *qaneh*, which means "measuring rod." The word came to mean "norm" or "rule," and evolved into the catalog or list of books we consider sacred.

852. It is sometimes assumed that the "canonization" of a book of Scripture meant that the Jewish nation or the Christian church "gave" authority to it. Instead, to canonize a book meant that Israel or the church recognized the authority of a book was already evident and ought to be recognized as such.

853. The two qualities of canonicity, as defined by the early church, were (1) that the teaching of a book was, in some unique sense, clearly divine; and (2) that the leadership of the church ascribed authority to it for all members.

854. The fact that the Books of the Law were recognized as being part of the Old Testament Canon is evident in that the tables of the Law were preserved in the ark of the covenant; the Book of the Law was kept by the side of the ark as a witness for God (see Deut. 31:24–26); and when the temple was renewed in the days of Josiah, the Scriptures were found hidden in the house of the Lord.

855. Moses commanded the people that the Books of the Law were to be read aloud to the people every seven years. The entire nation of Israel was to gather together so that every man, woman, and child would hear the Scriptures and be reminded of all God had done for them. (For details, see Deut. 31:10–13.)

856. The importance of the Old Testament law is made clear in 2 Chronicles 17:9, when the people were all urged to "obey" them. The king was to keep a copy by his side, to help guide his decisions. The Scriptures make it clear that the capture of Israel and Judah was caused by the people disobeying God's plain Word.

857. The New Testament Canon was formally recognized at the Third Council of Carthage in A.D. 397, but Christian churches had long before realized that some books stood on a plane of authority not shared by other books. The people were given spiritual discernment to enable them to determine the false books from the true.

858. The credibility of the Scriptures is evidenced by a comparison of facts. Nothing in the Bible is clearly contradictory to well-established facts of science. Archaeology has proven that the people, places, and events described in the Bible are found exactly where Scripture locates them. Facts about history, chronology, and ethnology are in complete harmony with the evidence of archaeology and historical records.

859. The Old Testament's first five books, the Pentateuch, were already considered authoritative Scripture by the time of Ezra in the fifth century B.C. The other books were recognized into the Old Testament at later times.

860. Jesus himself knew the "old covenant." As a Jewish boy, he diligently studied the Torah, Prophets, and Writings. He could cite them by heart when he was twelve. Because there was no Bible as we know it, he would have learned by rote from scrolls kept by local teachers or "rabbis."

861. The earliest references to the Old Testament were "the Law of Moses," "the Law of the Lord," or simply "Moses." Since the additional writings were considered the work of prophets, the common term came to be "Moses and the Prophets" or something similar. Note: wherever the word "law" is seen, the Jewish reference would be "torah." By New Testament times, "Scripture" or "the Scriptures" became common. The simplest generic term for the collection was Writings, often with "sacred" or "holy" added.

862. The uniformity of Bible printing sometimes obscures the scope of variety within the Bible's writings. If Bible printers laid out the print with all the different styles accounted for, a wheelbarrow would be needed to move a Bible from the den to the bedroom.

863. No Bible writer whom we know of ever drew a map to accompany his writing—at least not one that managed to get preserved. Maps are drawn from facts discovered through historical and archaeological research.

25

Interesting Ideas

864. The followers of the Astara religion teach that the Holy Spirit is the *Nahd*, or "holy sound current." In this role, they claim the Spirit presents "no creeds, dogmas, nor precepts which bind the mind in any way." In other words, every religion is right, no matter what dumb thing they proclaim!

865. Baha'i reject God as completely unknowable, regardless of what he has done in history. However, their founder, a man who called himself "Baha'u'llah," is more or less a divine figure. He once wrote, "Verily if I declare the right to be left, or the south to be north, it is true and there is no doubt therein." He also decreed, in his "secret" writings, that he discovered "the Greatest name is Baha'u'llah."

866. The religion of Buddhism is interesting in that it was originally atheistic, rejecting the reality of God, but later became polytheistic, claiming there are thousands of gods. Rejecting Jesus because they do not believe in a Savior (or even a need for salvation), they claim that this world is nothing more than an illusion, created in the minds of individuals.

867. Edgar Cayce, an influential mystic of the early 1900s, claimed to go into trances in which he received "the akashic records"—which is to say, purported wisdom from other-worldly beings. One of those tidbits of information was that the members of the Trinity are actually "Time, Space, and Patience."

868. The Christadelphian church got started the way most cults do—a man went into his barn with a Bible and came out six months later, claiming to have found the "new truth." Christadelphians superficially reject the Trinity because "the word does not appear in the Bible." However, *many* words which are true don't appear in Scripture (including "monotheism").

869. Mary Baker Eddy, a spirit medium who founded the Christian Science church, wrote, "We have no more proof of human sin . . . than we have that the earth's surface is flat and her motions imaginary." Claiming that man is god, death nonexistent, and Satan a myth, Baker (who loved wordplay) thought it significant that "God" and "good" contained the same letters. She said nothing about the fact that "God" and "dog" do also.

870. The Free Communion Church follows the writings of Franklin Jones, who refers to himself as "Da Free John," and claims to disseminate "the Way of Divine Ignorance." He is on record as calling himself God, arguing that all existence is garbage, and for sayings such as, "True wisdom is the capacity for madness."

871. The Divine Life Society is the official name of Swami Satchidananda's yoga organizations. The swami once claimed, "I am a true Christian, a true Muslim, a true Hindu, a true Buddhist, a true Sikh, and a true Parsi"—apparently unaware that at least *some* of those things are mutually exclusive. To yoga proponents, God is not a person but a state of "bliss."

872. Maharaj Ji, who broke away to start his own yoga outfit and is most famous for being pudgy and smoking marijuana with the Beatles, once quoted Scripture by saying, "Be still and know that I am God," and then adding his own flavoring: "Be still and know that *you* are god . . . for in stilling the mind is found salvation." Ji claims that "sin is forgiven by meditation."

873. Eckankar is a religion founded by Paul Twitchell, Darwin Gross, and Harold Klemp—three guys who claim to be the most recent in a six-million-year line of "living ECK masters." Depicting God as impersonal, amoral, and pantheistic, and likewise Jesus as a "son of the devil," they nevertheless claim themselves to be divine.

874. David Berg, who started the "Children of God" and refers to himself as everything from "Moses" to "King David," claimed that everything he wrote—even his papers for a business correspondence course—were inspired by God. Rejecting the Christian God as immoral, Berg once asked, "Where are God's witches? Where are His wizards? . . . They're here. It's *you!*"

875. The Holy Order of Mans, which uses everything from Tarot cards to psychic readings in order to find "wisdom," claims that Jesus Christ was an extremely advanced mystic who must have attained perfection. In recent years, one group has broken away and embraced biblical Christianity; another has moved into the Eastern Orthodox Church, renamed themselves "Christ the Savior Brotherhood," and made claims that the increasing interest in psychic stuff will herald the second coming.

876. Est, the Forum, Lifespring, Actualizations, and Silva Mind Control are all "human potential" seminars, claiming to present secrets of unlocking your inner power. They present the typical range of quasireligious thinking (God is within you; sin is a myth; you need to develop your psychic powers). But in recent years, one former follower, Daniel Tocchini, has molded this training into a "Christian" version he calls "Momentus." It's proven popular in churches throughout (surprise!) California.

877. The Jehovah's Witnesses is a cult that teaches the second coming occurred in 1874 (later changed to 1914), but that its arrival was "invisible." They believe Jesus is a created angel who first appeared as Michael the Archangel, later morphed into Jesus of Nazareth, and now exists as an exalted Michael. Their teaching also claims that Jesus wasn't born the Christ—instead he "became" the Christ when he got baptized.

878. The Lucis Trust views God as indefinable energy, ever evolving into some sort of advanced cosmic being. Like most cults, they base their beliefs on the unique interpretations of one person (in this case, Alice Bailey), subscribe to psychic development, believe that man can become God, view sin as nothing more than ignorance, and believe that Jesus was some sort of enlightened occult initiate.

879. Mormons believe that God is nothing more than an exalted man—in fact, they claim that the God of the Old Testament was created by the sexual union of a divine mother and father, and that he is merely the God of this earth, since there are potentially an infinite number of other gods. Early Mormonism taught that God was originally Adam who fell in the Garden of Eden (which, by the way, was located in Missouri, in case you hadn't heard).

880. The Mighty I AM, a small "Christian" cult, believes that God is "Saint Germain." They also list "Guy Ballard" as equal to Jesus in being an ascended master . . . Guy Ballard being the pen name of Godfre Ray King, who started the group.

881. Like most New Age groups, the New Thought Church rejects the personal God of the Bible in order to proclaim an impersonal "Universal Law" that is the essence of God. They view Jesus as a great man who realized his potential and oneness with God, and point to that as their hope that all men have a piece of the Almighty residing within them.

882. The "Jesus only" groups, particularly the members of the United Pentecostal Church, deny the Trinity as a "doctrine of demons." They baptize and pray "in the name of Jesus only," claiming that Matthew 28:19 demands believers to do so in "one name" (and conveniently ignoring the words of Christ himself). They reject the biblical account of Christ's preexistence and incarnation, insist on interpreting the Bible only through their own literature, and deny the personality and deity of the Holy Spirit.

883. Bhagwan Shree Rajneesh wrote that "obedience to God is the greatest sin," insisted that "Jesus is a mental case. . . . He carries the same mind as Adolf Hitler . . ." and declared that "my ashram makes no difference between the devil and the divine."

884. Richard Alpert, who started the Hanuman Foundation and went by the religious-sounding name "Ram Dass," claimed that "God came to the United States in the form of LSD." In one of his popular books about Eastern mysticism, he noted that "Krishna, Christ, Durga, Kali—all of them [are] the same." Then he offered this insightful analysis: "Different strokes for different folks."

885. "Who is Christ? He is *not* the only begotten Son of God"—the words of Ernest Holmes, founder of Religious Science. Rather than seeing Jesus as God, Holmes claimed Jesus expertly understood secret principles and thereby "became Christ conscious."

886. Rosicrucians offer a unique take on the Holy Spirit— they view him as "the Race god," who started Western thinking by pitting one race against another.

887. Those in the Ruhani Satsang hold to one of the strangest views of God in existence: they believe God is "sound" and refer to him as "the Divine Vibration."

888. The followers of Sai Baba believe him to be divine—literally the embodiment of "the second coming of Christ." This despite the fact that Baba, while claiming to make objects appear from nowhere, has been caught on tape relying on simple magic tricks to try and deceive his disciples into believing he has magical powers.

889. Scientology, trendy in Hollywood circles, was founded by science fiction writer L. Ron Hubbard. They believe people's souls have existed for eternity, that they are constantly being reincarnated, and that God is merely the term we use to refer to all life.

890. The Self-Realization Fellowship, another Buddhist-based cult, came up with a new take on the Trinity—they claim that the Father is "bliss," the Son is "universal consciousness," and the Spirit is "cosmic vibration." To get in touch with him, they use everything from mantras and yoga to channeling and divination.

891. Sikh, a form of the Hindu faith, rejects the divinity of Jesus, but at the same time claims that "god" is simply "knowing yourself." In the words of their guru, "To know thyself is to know God."

892. The Sufi Order claims to be the "original religion of God" (why God would *need* a religion isn't exactly clear). Their belief system argues that *everything* is God—every person, every action, every word, every animal, every plant. That's why one of their leaders, Meher Baba, can humbly declare, "I am God."

893. Emanuel Swedenborg (1688–1772) claimed to re-create the "one true Christian religion" when he started a church based on spiritism and talking to the dead. A brilliant scientist and inventor (Swedenborg designed airplanes and submarines more than one hundred years before their invention), he rejected orthodox teaching about God, encouraged occultic activity, and claimed humankind is "the symbol for God."

894. Helene Petrovna Blavatsky (1831–1891), the founder of Theosophy, claimed to have psychic powers and ancient wisdom given her by the gods. Her most famous spectacle was occasionally having letters flutter down from the ceiling of her home, suddenly appearing as though from another dimension. Unfortunately, the housekeeper, Emma Coulomb, later admitted to writing the letters and dropping them through a crack in the ceiling. The *Society for Psychical Research* examined Blavatsky's claims in 1884 and produced a two-hundred-page report that concluded she was a blatant fraud.

895. While the media has made a big deal about the Dalai Llama and his purported deep spirituality, the theology of Tibetan Buddhism is nontheistic—that is to say, they don't believe God exists, except as an undifferentiated and impersonal "universal mind."

896. UFOlogists (those who believe in UFOs) have generally formed their own unique theology in recent years. According to their belief system, visitors from other planets are abducting people and (even though these visitors are supposedly extremely creative and intelligent) drawing designs in crop fields. The theology is almost always the same: an impersonal God exists; Jesus was a great man but isn't God; humankind is basically good and has limitless potential; and creatures from space need to bring us wisdom and salvation because current religion doesn't contain the truth.

897. Sun Moon, the founder of the Unification Church, is famous for saying inanities such as, "As soon as a person believes in Jesus, Satan can invade his body" and "Your green bills are crying; if you want to make them happy, give them to the Father" (i.e., "hand over your money to me"). He views God as a being who has trouble controlling his own emotions, and who is dependent on man for his well-being. However, one of his most unique ideas is that the Holy Spirit is a woman.

898. The Unitarian Universalist Church is probably best known for allowing its members to accept (or reject) almost any belief system. But Jack Mendelsohn, an influential UU writer in the 1960s, noted that the God of the Bible is "a brutal deity . . . a monstrous being" and referred to the Lord as "demented."

899. Victor Paul Wierwille, who founded "the Way International" and takes out advertisements in college newspapers promising "personal power, success, health, and happiness" to those who join his cult, not only argues that Jesus was merely a man, but denies the virgin birth and claims that Christ was sent as the "replacement" for Lucifer!

26

Concepts and Doctrine

900. The Heidelberg Catechism was written in Germany at the request of the pious Christian Prince Frederick III, who ruled Heidelberg from 1559 to 1576. The prince asked two men, Zacharius Ursinus and Caspar Olevianus, to prepare a document that would instruct the youth and guide pastors and teachers as to the teachings of the Christian faith. Both men were under thirty years of age when the request was made, yet both were well versed in theology, Ursinus serving as a professor of theology at Heidelberg University and Olevianus acting as the prince's pastor.

901. A catechism is a summary of the principles of Christianity given in a question-and-answer format. The statements use Bible texts as proof of their truth. The idea was (and remains) that listeners were to take to heart and memory the statements of their faith and beliefs. The Heidelberg Catechism was first published in 1563 but went on to be published again (in German and Latin) with new additions that same year. The entire document was divided into fifty-two individual sections shortly after publication in order that one section of the catechism could be explained each week of the year, enabling a church to cover the catechism consistently.

902. Perhaps one of the most poignant statements of God's existence can be found in the first question of the Heidelberg Catechism: "What is your only comfort in life and in death?" The answer: "That I am not my own, but belong—body and soul, in life and in death—to my faithful Savior Jesus Christ. He has fully paid for all my sins with his precious blood, and has set me free from the tyranny of the devil. He also watches over me in such a way that not a hair can fall from my head without the will of my Father in heaven: in fact, all things must work together for my salvation. Because I belong to him, Christ, by his Holy Spirit, assures me of eternal life and makes me whole-heartedly willing and ready from now on to live for him."

903. Another catechism, the Westminster Catechism, came out of the request of the Westminster Assembly, which was assembled by the English parliament in 1643. The purpose was very similar to that of the Heidelberg Catechism—to educate the people sitting in the churches in a forthright manner about the principles of their faith. Two versions of this document emerged, the first in 1647 and the longer version a year later—a larger form for pulpit exposition. The first one remains in use today in many churches. It is loved by many for its direct focus and the ease in memorizing it over the larger form. The larger one has fallen into disuse.

904. The Westminster Catechism is structured on a two-part system: (1) What we are to believe concerning God, and (2) what duty God requires of us. The first part explains the basic teaching on God's nature as well as his creative and redemptive work. The second section covers the Ten Commandments, the doctrines of faith and repentance, the means of grace (reading the Word, celebrating the sacraments, prayer), and an explanation of the Lord's Supper.

905. The first question of the Westminster Shorter Catechism reads: "What is the chief end of man?" The answer: "The chief end of man is to glorify God and to enjoy Him forever."

906. Salvation is by grace. The most unique concept in the Christian faith is the fact that we do not *earn* our salvation by our good works. In fact, our good works contribute nothing to our standing with God. Instead salvation is a free gift from God, given to those who choose to follow him.

907. "Original sin" means "sinful from one's origin." Essentially Christians believe that we are born sinful and therefore incapable of becoming cleansed from our sins of our own abilities. Though this phrase is not mentioned in the Bible, Paul speaks of it somewhat in Romans. Original sin is a part of our human condition that can only be helped by the intercessory work of Jesus Christ. This idea originated with the first person ever placed on earth—Adam. Adam disobeyed God, an act that alienated him from God and caused all of his offspring to inherit his spiritual condition.

908. We were made in the "image of God." Even though we are all bound by original sin, we were made spiritually to resemble God. Through Christ's atoning work, a person can have a restored relationship with God, and through the Holy Spirit, we can put on the new person God has made us to be, resembling God more than ever before.

909. The idea of election is clear in Matthew 22, John 6, and Ephesians 1, as well as other places in the Bible. The Scripture teaches that certain individuals are given an inward experience through the Holy Spirit, imparting a sense of personal sin and inclining them toward repentance and faith in Jesus Christ. At the same time, *everyone* is invited to participate in the life of God, and his mercy is demonstrated to all. We are condemned as sinners, but the sovereign Lord shows leniency to some.

910. Atonement means to bring two distinct, individual things together in order to make them connect into one. In the Old Testament, the Israelites constantly offered sacrifices in order to "reconnect" with God as a result of their sins. In the New Testament, Christ came in order to be the final sacrifice for all people's sins. His death on the cross is often referred to as *"the* atonement" since it is the only sacrifice that completely and finally reconciles humanity with God.

911. Justification means "to make valid" or "to right," bringing righteousness. Because Jesus was a perfect man and completely without sin, those who believe in him and repent of their sins can be made righteous in God's sight. Becoming righteous is a free gift of God; with it a person is covered with Christ's atoning work so that the penalty for their sins is removed.

912. Sanctification means to "make holy." This is a work of the Holy Spirit within us after a Christian has been justified. Sanctification is the putting on of the new person that a believer has become as a result of believing in Jesus Christ and having faith in his atoning work. Sincere Christians want to stop sinning, to become more like Christ in their daily work and life. The Holy Spirit who now lives in them helps new believers to do this.

913. Covenants are a very important aspect to keep in mind when reading the Bible. A covenant is an "agreement between two or more parties." The Bible is especially about those covenants made between God and man. The agreements were formal and were a demonstration of God's continued faithfulness to those with whom he made the agreements.

914. The rainbow was a sign of the first covenant God made with his people. Noah and his family were the only ones to survive the flood; God told them he would never again cause such a flood to happen. The sign of his promise was the rainbow. Man wasn't required to do anything—it was a promise of God to all creation that he would spare humankind from a worldwide flood.

915. The circumcision covenant made between Abraham and God directly affected all the male descendants of Abraham, who was considered the father of the Israelites (Genesis 17). All were required to undergo the surgical procedure. Those males who did not become circumcised were considered outsiders of the covenant and were banished from their people. Circumcision was a sign that the Israelites were God's special people, "the people of the covenant."

916. When the Israelites reached Mount Sinai on their way to Canaan (after leaving Egypt), Moses gave them the laws that had been given to him by God. The people were brought into the Sinai Covenant at this time: If they would obey the laws of God, he would bless them and settle his people in the land of Canaan. However, if they disobeyed, they would suffer the consequences. The law Moses gave the people included a system of sacrifices they were to use in order to show their repentance of sins. God did not expect perfection of his people, only obedient hearts who were willing to follow him.

917. Another covenant was made with the Israelites after they were carried into exile in Babylon as a result of breaking the Sinai Covenant. This new covenant was prophesied by Jeremiah and stated that God would put his law into the people's hearts and minds so that they would want to serve him. The people thus would obey God and want to please him, and God would continue to love the Israelites and take care of them (Jer. 31:33).

918. The New Covenant was made when Christ died and became the atoning sacrifice for all who choose to repent and believe. As Jesus himself states, the old covenant was no longer applicable: "This is my blood of the new covenant, which is shed for many" (Mark 14:24 NKJV). Christ's death was the ultimate sacrifice and did away with the old system of law God had given to his people at Sinai.

919. Baptism is one of two sacraments or ordinances of the Christian church. It is the act of using water to demonstrate a person's cleansing from sin by Jesus Christ's atoning work. It is a symbol of one's being "signed and sealed" in the forgiveness of Jesus Christ and follows God's covenant of the Old Testament regarding circumcision. As baptized Christians, we are designated God's people. Some people believe in infant baptism, while others believe a person should be old enough to make a conscious decision about this practice. Baptism is purely a symbol—people are not made into Christians by its practice.

920. The Lord's Supper, or communion, is the other sacrament of the Christian church. Christians come together in their church services and celebrate communion as a reminder of Jesus' Last Supper. Partaking of the wine and bread, which is what Jesus partook of in the upper room with his disciples the night he was betrayed, is a symbol of our sharing in Christ's suffering. Jesus told his disciples when he ate those elements, "This is my body (my blood), which is given for you, do this in remembrance of me." Jesus' atoning work on the cross as a sacrifice for our sins is the reason we may have forgiveness; the church celebrates the Lord's Supper in memory of it.

921. The body of Christ is the earthly church. The idea behind this metaphor is that a fellowship of believers is a living, tangible being with all different parts (people) working together to function as one unit. The apostle Paul states that Christ is the head of the body and leads it, and that "each member belongs to all the others" (Rom. 12:5).

922. Evangelism means "good news" and comes from the New Testament word *euangelion*. The "good news" is a reference to the message of Christ's redemptive work for our sins. Sharing this message with others was a direct result of Christ's instruction to his disciples: the Great Commission. The universal church is to share this message with those who have not heard about what Jesus did for them.

923. Excommunication is a biblical and Christian concept for dealing with those who are unrepentant, heretical, or living in a state of sin while also maintaining a profession of being a Christian. It is not a tool to be used quickly or taken lightly. Those in the church who are leaders use it as the final step in dealing with an unrepentant Christian. After an initial path of going to the person privately with the matter to seek understanding, then taking the case to the church authorities, who will also try to pray, counsel, and reason with the person, the Bible says, if they continue in unrepentance, to refuse them a place to worship. Excommunication is not an end all either. People who have been excommunicated have also come to repentance and been welcomed back with open arms by those in the church who originally cast them out. It is also not a method of shunning. Christians are not called to ignore the person should they see her or him, and all in the church are generally encouraged to pray for the person.

924. The tribulation is a period during the end times when evil will be running wild, before God triumphs over Satan. Jesus spoke of this time in the Book of Matthew: "For then shall be great tribulation, such as was not since the beginning of the world to this time, no, nor ever shall be" (24:21 KJV). This time of persecution that is spoken of in Revelation 7:14 is called the "great tribulation." Christians have taken that word and used it as a reference to this time. Some theorize that the tribulation is already underway, citing those many Christians who have died of persecution since the beginning of the church.

925. The millennium is a time period of a thousand years. In Revelation 20, the Bible speaks of a thousand-year reign of Christ on earth. During this time, Satan will be bound and unable to do any evil on earth. However, Satan will be released at some point, but then he will be defeated forever. Three main views are held by Christians regarding this time period.

926. Postmillennialism is the belief that the Christian faith is expanding, thus continually improving the world. Throughout the eighteenth and nineteenth centuries, theologians posited that the "church era" would eventually bring all things under the headship of Christ, ushering in an era of peace that would last for a thousand years.

927. Premillennialism isn't a new invention. Manuel de Lacunza, a Chilean monk in the mid-1700s, was the first modern scholar to suggest a premillennial return of Christ. Lacunza said the world would head toward destruction, but that Christ would appear and remove his faithful from the worst of it (the tribulation), before returning to establish his one-thousand-year reign. Written during a time of almost universal postmillennialism, Lacunza's words were ignored for almost two centuries.

928. Amillennialism has been around longer than either of its counterparts. The Book of Revelation is read as symbolic rather than literal, and the coming of the kingdom of God is a two-part event. The first part began when Christ came to earth and continues even now; for the amillennialist, the final things are essentially accomplished already, though not by sight but by faith. The second part will begin at his second coming. Christ is ruling on high in the present age, which is seen as being symbolic of the thousand-year reign discussed in Revelation. Evil is fully present (note Christ's parable of the wheat and the tares growing next to each other), but Christ is dominant. The kingdom of God is present through the church, but this is not a presence that is moving toward fulfillment because fulfillment will come with the glory of heaven, not with the earthly church.

929. Dispensationalism is a method of viewing the history of how God has dealt with his people, beginning with Adam in the Garden of Eden. In this theory, there are seven time periods (dispensations) in history. The seventh dispensation includes the return of Christ. Dispensationalists believe God has used varying methods to deal with humans, depending on the dispensation currently being experienced. The current time period would be the sixth dispensation, which is the age of the church. With this method comes a tendency to disregard the Old Testament (and sometimes parts of the New Testament) as being out-of-date or unapplicable as those were different periods of time and required a different approach.

930. The second coming refers to when Christ will return to earth to be with his people. Though this phrase is not used in the Bible, Jesus spoke of his return in the Gospels of Matthew and John. The New Testament authors all spoke of staying alert, of being prepared as no one knows "the day or the hour" when Christ will return.

27

An Eternal Purpose

931. The decrees of God may be defined as God's eternal purpose (in a real sense, all things are embraced in one purpose) or purposes, based on his most wise and holy counsel, whereby he ordained (appointed or predetermined) all that comes to pass. With infinite power and infinite wisdom, God has from all eternity past decided and chosen and determined the course of all events.

932. His decrees . . .

> reveal God's eternal purpose;
> are based on his most wise and holy counsel;
> originate in his freedom;

are a result of his omnipotent desires;

have as their end his glory; and

embrace all that comes to pass.

933. The two kinds of decrees. There are things that God purposes through his power to bring about; there are other things that he merely determines to permit (Rom. 8:28). But even in the case of the permissive decrees, God rules over all things for his glory (Matt. 18:7; Acts 2:23).

934. Proof of the decrees. The events in the universe are neither a surprise nor a disappointment to God, nor the result of his impulsive or random will. Instead they are the outworking of a definite purpose and plan of God as taught in Scripture: The Lord of hosts has sworn saying, "Surely, just as I have intended so it has happened, and just as I have planned so it will stand, . . . For the Lord of hosts has planned, and who can frustrate it? And as for His stretched-out hand, who can turn it back?" (Isa. 14:24, 27 NASB).

935. Reasons for God's actions. Why was God not content to confine his fellowship and activity to the Trinity? We are assured that God always has reasons for his actions (Deut. 29:29). "Later you will understand" (John 13:7) is encouraging in that we will someday understand the meaning of certain puzzling Scriptures and the mysteries of certain perplexing acts of God.

936. The highest aim of the decrees is the glory of God. Creation glorifies him. David says, "The heavens declare the glory of God; the skies proclaim the work of his hands" (Ps. 19:1). When God declares that he will refine Israel in the furnace of affliction, he adds, "For my own sake, for my own sake, I do this. How can I let myself be defamed? I will not yield my glory to another" (Isa. 48:11).

937. Seeking glory. For humanity to seek glory would be selfishness, but that is because we are sinful and imperfect. To seek for such glory would be to seek to glorify sinfulness and imperfection. But this is not the case with God. He is absolutely sinless and perfect in holiness. For him to aim at his own glory is, therefore, merely to seek the glory of absolute holiness and sinless perfection. There is no one and nothing higher to glorify. We must aim in everything to glorify him who is the manifestation of all goodness, purity, wisdom, and truth.

938. God has decreed all that has come to pass in the material and physical realm, in the moral and spiritual realm, and in the social and political realm.

939. God decreed to create the universe and humankind. He decreed to establish the earth. He also decreed never again to destroy the population of the earth by means of a universal flood. He distributed the nations, appointed their seasons, and set the bounds of their habitation. He also decreed the length of human life and the manner of our exit from this life. All the other events in the material and physical realm have likewise been decreed and are in God's plan and purpose.

940. God's decrees in the moral and spiritual realm leave us with two basic problems: the existence of evil in the world and the freedom of humanity. How can a holy God allow moral evil, and how can a sovereign God permit man to be free?

941. God determined to permit sin. Though God is not the author of sin (James 1:13–14), and didn't necessitate it, he did, on the basis of his wise and holy counsel, decree to permit the fall and sin to come. God did this in light of what he knew would be the nature of sin, of what he knew sin would do to his creation. And he knew all that would have to be done to redeem humanity from their sin. God could have prevented it, but he chose instead to gift his creatures—angels and mankind—with a free will. "In the generations gone by He permitted all the nations to go their own ways" (Acts 14:16 NASB).

942. He determined to overrule sin for good. This determination is inseparable from the one to permit sin. But God is sovereign, holy, and wise and he cannot permit sin to thwart his purposes. It must be overruled for good. Joseph said to his brothers, "You meant evil against me, but God meant it for good in order to bring about this present result, to preserve many people alive" (Gen. 50:20 NASB). The psalmist said, "The LORD foils the plans of the nations; he thwarts the purposes of the peoples. But the plans of the LORD stand firm forever, the purposes of his heart through all generations" (Ps. 33:10–11).

943. God determined to save mankind from sin. All Christians are agreed that God has decreed to save humanity, but not all are agreed as to *how* he does so. We must remember that (1) God must take the initiative in salvation, (2) humanity, even in our present helpless state, is responsible, and (3) God's decrees are not based on random or arbitrary decisions, but rather on his wise and holy counsel. Some see election as dependent upon divine foreknowledge, others see election and foreknowledge, as they relate to saving faith, as essentially inseparable.

944. The "plan of God" or the "will of God" refers not only to all events in history, but all human actions, all the affairs of nations, and even the period of human life. Each man's and woman's birth, death, and salvation are part of God's plan.

945. God "calls" or "invites" all to know him. Some believe that God has called only the elect to know him. Others believe there is a general invitation for all people to be saved, and it is given through the Word of God. That said, it is understood that not all people will be saved.

946. God determined to reward his servants and to punish the disobedient. Although God is active and demonstrates grace to both believers and unbelievers, he does promise to care for his children and to never forget them. That cannot be said for the disobedient who do not follow him.

947. A severe love is what distinguishes the difference between the Father giving Christ over for execution, Jesus delivering himself, and Judas betraying Christ to the authorities for thirty pieces of silver. As Augustine of Hippo once said, "What the Father and the Son did in love, Judas did in treacherous betrayal. . . . God had in mind our redemption, Judas had in mind the price for which he sold Jesus. Jesus himself, had in mind the price He gave for us. . . . Love must sometimes show itself severe."

948. God's decrees in the social and political realm include the family and the home. In the very beginning, God said, "It is not good for the man to be alone; I will make him a helper suitable for him" (Gen. 2:18). By the fact that God made one man and only one woman, he indicated that marriage was to be monogamous and indissoluble (Matt. 19:3–9). All through the Scriptures, the sanctity of marriage is recognized. The decree of marriage implies the decree to have and to establish a home.

949. The decree of human government is closely related to that of the family. God has by decree determined the location, season, and boundaries of the nations. He has likewise ordained the rulers of the nations (Dan. 4:34–37; Rom. 13:1–7). All rulers are to recognize the sovereign rule of God and to seek to carry out his will (Ps. 2:10–12). If the ruler chooses not to and makes laws contrary to the commandments of God, the subjects are to obey God rather than the human ruler (Acts 4:19; 5:29).

950. The call and mission of Israel began when God chose Abraham to be the leader of his chosen people (Gen. 12:1–3). God then limited the bloodline after Abraham to Isaac, Jacob, and the twelve sons of Jacob. God chose Israel for himself, to make them a kingdom of priests, and a holy nation (Exod. 19:4–6). When Israel miserably failed God, the natural branches were broken off and the Gentiles, signified by branches of a wild olive tree, were grafted into the stem (Rom. 11:11–22). Someday God will graft in again the natural branches (Rom. 11:23–27).

951. The founding and mission of the church came about when Jesus declared that he would build his church (Matt. 16:18), indicating that it was not yet in existence at that time. Paul declared that while the church was included in God's eternal purpose, the nature of it was not fully revealed until Jesus' day (Eph. 3:1–13).

952. The final triumph of God will occur when the Father gives all the kingdoms of the world to Christ (Ps. 2:6–9; Dan. 7:13–14; Luke 1:31–33; Rev. 11:15–17; 19:11–20:6). In connection with his taking over these kingdoms, there will be the "regeneration" of nature (Matt. 19:27–30; Rom. 8:19–22). His rule will be characterized by peace and righteousness (Ps. 2:8–12; Isa. 9:6–7). This first phase of God's triumph on the earth will last for a period of a thousand years (Rev. 20:1–6). After Satan's final revolt and the great white throne judgment (Rev. 20:7–15) will come the new heavens, new earth, and the New Jerusalem (Rev. 21:1–22:5). Then Christ will deliver up the kingdom of God, even the Father; and the triune God—Father, Son, and Holy Spirit—will reign forever and ever (1 Cor. 15:23–28). All of these things were decreed by God and will come to pass.

953. The core of God's plan is to rescue us from sin. Our pain, poverty, and broken hearts are not his ultimate focus. . . . God cares most about teaching us to hate our sins, grow up spiritually, and love him. People's illnesses weren't Jesus' focus—the gospel was. His miracles were a backdrop, a visual aid, to his urgent message. Jesus' message was: Sin will kill you, hell is real, God is merciful, his kingdom will change you, and I am your passport.

28

How Can We Find Him?

954. Having faith in God is the first step to understanding him. We must believe he exists before we can go any further. The first four words of Genesis make it clear that God was in the beginning: "In the beginning God. . . ."

955. There must also be a belief that God can be known—that he can be found—in order to have faith in him. As described later, two kinds of revelation make this possible, general and special revelation. Romans 1:19–20 says, "What may be known about God is plain to them, because God has made it plain to them. For since the creation of the world God's invisible qualities—his eternal power and divine nature—have been clearly seen, being understood from what has been made, so that men are without excuse."

956. There must be a belief in the rationality of God. This is not to say that we believe it is possible to understand exactly why God does things the way he does; God is a deity and far beyond the knowledge of man. However, from the Bible and from God's promises, we can know that he acts for our greater good and honors his covenants. He is an orderly God, a knowledgeable God, a God of reason.

957. A final necessity for finding faith in God is the need to believe in the character of God. A biblical faith rests on the philosophy that God is sovereign, omnipresent, loving, just, righteous, and unchanging from age to age. We know God to be faithful to us by his continual care for his people and by how he has accepted us after we repent of our sins.

958. Revelation is the act of God whereby he discloses himself, or communicates truth to the mind, of things that could not be known in any other way. Theologians often refer to two different types of God's revelation: general and special.

959. God is revealed in nature. The earth reveals that there is a God and that he has such attributes as power, glory, divinity, and goodness. General revelation draws humanity to search for a fuller revelation of God and his plan of salvation. The psalmists, prophets, and apostles expressed the revelation of God through nature (Job 12:7–9; Ps. 8:1–3; 19:1–3; Isa. 40:12–14, 26; Acts 14:15–17; Rom. 1:19–20).

960. God is revealed in conscience. The human conscience judges whether an action or attitude is in harmony with our moral standard, and urges us to make the right choice. The presence in humanity of this sense of right and wrong reveals the existence of God. The conscience is the reflection of God in the soul. Just as a mirror or the smooth surface of a lake reflects the sun and not only reveals its existence, but also to some extent its nature, so conscience in man reveals both the existence of God and, to some extent, the nature of God.

961. God is revealed in history. The Christian finds a revelation of God's power and providence throughout ancient and recent history. The apostle Paul declares that God has "made from one man every nation of mankind to live on all the face of the earth, having determined their appointed times and the boundaries of their habitation, that they would seek God, if perhaps they might grope for Him and find Him" (Acts 17:26–27 NASB). History became, in Bonhoeffer's phrase, "the womb of the birth of God."

962. God personally appeared to the patriarchs, making himself and his will known in dreams and visions, and communicating his message directly to them. At a time when the whole world had sunk into polytheism and pantheism, Abraham, Isaac, Jacob, and their descendants came to know God as a personal, infinite, holy, and self-revealing God (see Josh. 24:2).

963. General revelation is the term used to describe the evidence of God as seen in the world. According to Psalm 19, "The heavens declare the glory of God; the skies proclaim the work of his hands. Day after day they pour forth speech; night after night they display knowledge. There is no speech or language where their voice is not heard" (vv. 1–3). In other words, God's presence is evident in nature.

964. In Acts 17:22–29, the apostle Paul argues that since God made the world, he is therefore bigger than the world. Furthermore, if mankind is truly his creation, then it is obvious God is personal rather than inanimate. A personal Creator would certainly not make an impersonal being. This is the type of "general revelation" that declares the reality of God.

965. The concept of general revelation is most obvious in nature (see Rom. 1:20). John Calvin once wrote that God has so manifested "his perfections in the whole structure of the universe . . . we cannot open our eyes without being compelled to behold him" (*Institutes of the Christian Religion,* 1.5.1).

966. The concept of general revelation also takes place *within* mankind. Since man is made in God's image, being personal and having a capacity for love, creativity, and history means we cannot escape the notion that man was created by a loving, creative God. And since man has a built-in ethical inclination, the theistic implication is that man holds the truth of his origin within himself, but continually attempts to suppress this indicator of the divine so that he can become his own God. Augustine, in *Confessions* 1.1.1, wrote, "Thou has formed us for Thyself, and our hearts are restless until they find rest in Thee."

967. The result of general revelation is that man is left without excuse before God. He cannot claim he was unaware of the reality of God, since the Lord is present both within and without man. No individual can escape the knowledge of God's reality unless he or she chooses to suppress or avoid the revelation of God in creation.

968. Special revelation is the term used to describe the unique ways God has chosen to reveal himself in history. Remember that God is transcendent—he exists beyond human comprehension. If he is to be known, it must happen outside the normal path of human understanding. God, in his divine will, *chooses* to make himself known to man. The methods that he uses are termed "special revelation."

969. Special revelation includes those acts of God whereby he makes himself and his truth known at special times and to specific peoples. Yet the revelation is not necessarily intended for that time and people only. The special revelation is a treasure to be shared with the whole world, according to Matthew 28:19–20. It is given to humanity in various ways: in the form of miracles, in prophecy, in the person and life of Jesus Christ, in the Scriptures, and in personal experience.

970. Since special revelation is given to save mankind from sin, the content of special revelation is the story of our salvation. Thus the most well-known means of special revelation—the Bible—details the relationship between God and humans.

971. Sometimes special revelation occurs as historical events. For example, the salvation of the Israelites from Egypt, their survival in the wilderness, and their capture of Jericho are all examples of special revelation. Miracles are demonstrations of God's power and point to his presence in the midst of humankind.

972. Another form of special revelation is the Bible. In it, God's very words reveal the truth of history, offering descriptions of God's redemptive acts throughout the ages. The Scriptures were given in order to help mankind recognize God, better understand him, and know how to develop a healthy relationship with him.

973. The Bible uses pictures and analogies to express the relationship in the manner of a son knowing his father, a wife knowing her husband, a subject knowing his king, and a sheep knowing its shepherd. This is the biblical concept of knowing God: Those to whom he allows himself to be known are loved and cared for by him.

974. The term "inspiration," when applied to the Bible, means that the writers of each book were empowered and controlled by the Holy Spirit in the production of the Scriptures. The hand of God is evident in the fact that each book has a divine, infallible authority.

975. "Internal proof" is the term used to describe the Bible's divine origin. The fact that forty different authors from several different countries, sharing almost no mutual acquaintance, wrote sixty-six books in three different languages over the course of two thousand years, yet produced essentially one book with one clear message is strong evidence that God was behind the writing of Scripture. Though some books were historical, others prophetical, some devotional, and still others ethical, yet the writers created one unified text. Its shared thoughts about God, man, sin, eternal punishment, and the mode of salvation are all strong proofs that the book is a revelation from God.

976. Sometimes the Word of God arrives *before* events occur, declaring that something will come to pass in the future. This is prophecy—an example of God being all-knowing by revealing the truth in advance. Prophecy is generally given to declare God's glory, to warn about future events, or to point people toward the Lord.

977. The New Testament in particular is the perpetuation of God's story. The words of the Gospels reveal Jesus Christ as the only avenue to God and the perfect extension of God's spoken word.

978. Jesus Christ is the epitome of special revelation. He is the supreme event in the revelation of God's will, God's love, and God's desire to redeem humanity. Jesus is the supreme expression of special revelation as historical event, since he is the center of all history.

979. "Soteriology" is the study of salvation. The word comes from the Greek word *soteria,* which means "salvation." Someone studying salvation would explore topics such as faith, repentance, justification, and regeneration.

980. Adam's sin makes salvation by God necessary. Sin brought death to the human race, and corrupted the entire universe. As a result, man is in need of redemption. Since man cannot save himself, a special act of God was necessary in order to bring about salvation.

981. We are saved by grace through faith in Jesus Christ, according to Ephesians 2:8–9. In Old Testament times, salvation was also offered as a gracious gift of God to those who had faith—as Genesis 15:6 puts it, "Abram believed the Lord, and he credited it to him as righteousness" (see also Gal. 3:8; Titus 2:11; Heb. 4:2; and 1 Peter 1:10–11).

982. The Hebrew word for "salvation" can also be translated "health" or "rescue," so the saving work of God *rescues* us from eternal punishment.

983. Christ paid the penalty for our sins when he died on the cross. As Romans 8:1 puts it, "Therefore, there is now no condemnation for those who are in Christ Jesus."

984. The word *salvation* refers not only to the moment an individual believes in Jesus, but also to the *process* of being sanctified. That's why Paul encourages believers to "continue to work out your salvation in fear and trembling" (Phil. 2:12).

985. Salvation has a future aspect, at which time we will be permanently changed, losing our old sin nature and becoming like Jesus (Rom. 8:22–23).

986. While salvation is given by faith, rather than by our works (see Rom. 3:28), our new life should manifest itself through good works (see James 2:22–24). As Paul put it in Ephesians 2:8–10, "For it is by grace you have been saved, through faith—and this not from yourselves, it is the gift of God—not by works, so that no one can boast. For we are God's workmanship, created in Christ Jesus to do good works."

987. Some critics have argued that Paul and James disagree with each other, since Paul focused on salvation by grace and James writes about the importance of works. However, a careful reading reveals that the two authors are exploring two different aspects of the faith. Paul presents God's view: we are saved by grace through faith. James presents the view from our perspective: true faith will demonstrate itself through good works.

988. The word *repentance* means literally "to change directions." Believers in Christ were once headed their own way but are now headed toward the Lord.

989. The word *justification* is a judicial term in which an individual is declared innocent by a judge. Since man is the sinner, God is the Judge. Although man is sinful and therefore guilty before God, in the case of the believer Christ's death on the cross is presented as the full payment for sin—thereby allowing the Judge to declare those under Christ's control as innocent.

990. *Sanctification* **means to be "set apart"** for something sacred. Believers in Jesus are *sanctified*—that is, they have been set apart from the evil in the world, for the purpose of having their lives point others to God (John 17:19–21).

991. Believers in Jesus are "adopted" into the family of God. That's why Jesus could call his disciples "brothers," and why the apostle John could declare, "How great is the love the Father has lavished on us, that we should be called children of God! And that is what we are!" (1 John 3:1).

992. Adoption was a Jewish custom that occurred when a child reached the age of twelve. At that time, the father would publicly declare he was "adopting" his natural-born son. In doing so, the father was declaring that the son was responsible for his own actions. God's "adoption" of believers is therefore a way of noting that his children are responsible to demonstrate their Father's character—in the words of Romans 8:29, "to be conformed to the likeness of his Son."

993. The blessings of salvation include forgiveness of sin, adoption as God's child, access to God, victory over sin, peace in our current world, and the future promise of eternity in heaven. Becoming a child of God is a process laid out in the Bible that remains true today.

994. A. W. Tozer gives seven steps for coming to a saving knowledge of God in his book *The Knowledge of the Holy*. As he says in preface to these, "As sunlight falls free on the open field, so the knowledge of the holy God is a free gift to men who are open to receive it. But this knowledge is difficult because there are conditions to be met and the obstinate nature of fallen man does not take kindly to them."

995. Step 1: Becoming a child of God requires us to forsake our sins. Our sin keeps us from a relationship with a holy, perfect God who is without sin. Jesus made reference to the need to be free of sin in order to be closer to God when he said, "Blessed are the pure in heart; for they will see God" (Matt. 5:8). There must be repentance and an acknowledgment of our complete inability to save ourselves. We must be "justified."

996. Step 2: After we have turned from our sins, there is a need to make a complete committal of our lives to Christ. Through a faith in him, we must "believe in Christ." Such a commitment requires both a personal, spiritual attachment to our Savior as well as an active intent to obey God in all matters.

997. Step 3: We must undergo this turning from our sin to the point that we die to sin and become alive to Jesus Christ. Furthermore, we must open our heart, soul, mind, and strength to the Holy Spirit, who will uphold us and comfort us as we begin growing in our faith. This process is called "sanctification."

998. Step 4: As we turn from sin, we must also turn from the fallen world that used to be our comfort. We must live lives dedicated to God that are absent of idolatry for what the world has to offer. Our lives should reflect a new commitment—a new focus.

999. Step 5: We must spend time in prayer and worship of God. God can be known in greater detail through communion with him, through study of his Word, and through reflection on his creation. Our personal relationship with God requires us to want to seek to know him more and more in order to continue to grow in him. The more we know him, the more we are likely to seek his will for our lives.

1000. Step 6: As we grow in our knowledge of God, we should have a greater desire to serve others as Christ taught us to. A natural response to God revealing himself to us includes demonstrating that knowledge in the way we live. Through greater knowledge of his abundant love and mercy, believers will automatically share that which has been given freely to them to others through kindness and love to our fellowmen. As Tozer states: "The God who gave all *to* us will continue to give all *through* us as we come to know Him better."

1001. Step 7: The final step breaks away from the pattern of the previous six. These dealt more with the personal relationship we have with God; the last step involves purposefully sharing this wonderful gift of God through active involvement in his church. Our light should be evident to all, but especially to our fellow believers in the Christian community.

Bibliography

The NIV Study Bible. Copyright © 1985 by The Zondervan Corporation.

Psalter Hymnal. Copyright ©1976 by the Board of Publications of the Christian Reformed Church, Inc., Grand Rapids.

Emery H. Bancroft. *Elemental Theology.* Grand Rapids: Zondervan, 1977.

Donald G. Bloesch. *God the Almighty: Power, Wisdom, Holiness, Love.* Downers Grove, Ill.: InterVarsity Press, 1995.

Ed Bulkley. *How Big Is Your God? Finding a Faith That Really Works.* Eugene, Oreg.: Harvest House, 1997.

Michael Caputo. *God Seen through the Eyes of the Greatest Minds.* West Monroe, La.: Howard Publishing, 2000.

M. R. DeHaan, M.D. *Portraits of Christ in Genesis.* Grand Rapids: Zondervan, 1966.

John R. de Witt. *What Is the Reformed Faith?* Carlisle, Pa.: Banner of Truth Trust, 1981.

Terry W. Glaspey. *Pathway to the Heart of God: Inspired to Pray by the Great Christian Writers.* Eugene, Oreg.: Harvest House, 1998.

Douglas Kelly and Philip Rollinson. *The Westminster Shorter Catechism in Modern English.* Phillipsburg, N.J.: Presbyterian and Reformed Publishing Co., 1986.

Stephen Lang. *1001 Things You Always Wanted to Know about the Bible but Never Thought to Ask.* Nashville: Thomas Nelson, 1999.

Jerry MacGregor and Marie Prys. *1001 Surprising Things You Should Know about the Bible.* Grand Rapids: Baker, 2002.

Arthur W. Pink. *The Attributes of God.* Grand Rapids: Baker, 1975.

Bruce Shelley. *Church History in Plain Language.* Dallas: Word, 1982.

Thomas Albert Stafford. *Christian Symbolism in the Evangelical Churches.* New York: Abingdon-Cokesbury Press, 1942.

A. W. Tozer. *The Knowledge of the Holy.* San Francisco: HarperCollins, 1961.

Index

237